W9-BYH-114

SOLE SISTERS

STORIES OF WOMEN AND RUNNING

Jennifer Lin and Susan Warner

Andrews McMeel
Publishing, LLC
Kansas City · Sydney · London

To our husbands and kids . . .
Bill, Karl, and Cory
—Jennifer Lin
Strauss, Ella, and Sylvia
—Susan Warner

Andrews McMeel Publishing, LLC
an Andrews McMeel Universal company
1130 Walnut Street, Kansas City, Missouri 64106

www.andrewsmcmeel.com

11 12 13 14 MLT 10 9 8 7 6

Library of Congress Cataloging-in-Publication Data
Lin, Jennifer.
    Sole sisters : stories of women and running / Jennifer Lin and Susan Warner.
        p. cm.
    ISBN: 978-0-7407-5711-2
        1. Women runners—Anecdotes. 2. Running for women—Anecdotes. I. Warner,
Susan, 1957– II. Title.

GV1061.10.W66L56 2006
796.42092—dc22
[B]

                                                                    2005057061

Design by Holly Camerlinck

Attention: Schools and Businesses

Andrews McMeel books are available at quantity discounts with bulk purchase for educational, business, or sales promotional use. For information, please e-mail the Andrews McMeel Publishing Special Sales Department:
specialsales@amuniversal.com

Contents

. . . . .

Why We Run

Like many women, our running started with a craving for ice cream. And creamy pasta. And dark chocolate. But before long, our three-mile jogs along Philadelphia's riverside Kelly Drive became so much more than a way to burn calories. It was our therapy, our time to mull questions big and small, to escape the workaday world, to connect, to talk. Eyes focused straight ahead, legs turning in tandem, we free-associated on everything from what to serve at a daughter's bat mitzvah to how to renovate a beach house. We commiserated over fussy cats and forgetful husbands, working our way up to the Rosetta stone of our beings, our mothers. We took turns and switched topics, one moment celebrating the success of a shy child on the soccer field or ballet stage, the next lamenting the creaks and gray hair of middle age. And across those miles, our running brought back the lost pleasure of visiting for a spell with a friend.

We weren't alone. On our midday runs, we passed a constant stream of women—running alone or in pairs—who seemed to easily outnumber male runners on Kelly Drive. What was going on? That question led to an article we cowrote for the *Philadelphia Inquirer* about the boom in women's running. Our ranks were growing: 11 million strong and counting. In response to the article, we got phone calls, letters, and e-mails from other runners who wanted to tell us why they run. Friends shared tales about women whose lives had been transformed through running. We began collecting stories. We talked to race organizers and running-store owners. We went online and found runners in other parts of the country to talk to—a cancer survivor in Albany, a nun in Northern California, a running-club organizer in St. Louis, a Cheyenne teenager from Montana, and a Boulder woman who runs with horses.

We share with you their stories, our stories. We are women who have discovered the joy of running and know that at the end of a good workout comes the mixed benefits of fitness and friendship . . . and maybe some ice cream, pasta, and dark chocolate.

CHAPTER 1

Joan
NESBIT MABE

A world-class racer turns coach of moms

The school fund-raiser couldn't have come at a more serendipitous time for Joan Nesbit Mabe. Her daughter's preschool needed donations for a silent auction. Joan offered her time. She auctioned a ten-week training program for runners with one hitch: Only mothers were allowed. It was meant to be a one-shot deal. It became so much more.

The year was 2000, a pivotal time for Joan. She was thirty-eight, remarried, and the mother of two daughters. She had been running competitively for two decades and could sense it was time to say good-bye to racing. That summer, she competed in her fifth Olympic Trials. She had made the U.S. squad for the 1996 Atlanta Games, running in the marquee 10,000 meters. This time around, at the 2000 trials, Joan finished in the middle of the pack in the 1,500 meters, content just to be part of the experience.

More and more, Joan wondered about the next phase of her life. Where would her running take her? She had climbed to the top of her sport. She had been a big-league college coach, once leading both the men's and women's cross-country teams at the University of North Carolina. She had worn red, white, and blue in the Olympics. She had records and titles.

Now what?

Luckily, motherhood left her little time to grieve for her fading status as a competitor. She had one daughter to potty train and another in Brownies. And right now, her daughter's school needed to raise money.

Around the preschool in Chapel Hill, North Carolina, Joan was known as "Rosie's mom"—not Joan the UNC track legend, two-time All-American, 1995 national cross-country champion, 1996 Olympian.

Just Rosie's mom.

The training program for the auction filled up quickly. Ten mothers signed on. Just enough, thought Joan. She had a reason for focusing on mothers. Joan remembered firsthand how isolated she felt as a new mother.

"I was the most lonely I've ever been," Joan recalls. "I used to wonder, 'Is anyone else feeling this way?'"

Joan had little support juggling the demands of motherhood and coaching (not to mention her own training) among the alpha males of college sports. At the same time, there were not many elite athletes like herself who were taking detours on the mommy track. Her running peers were incredulous when she decided to interrupt training and competing to have her first daughter in 1993. One rival pronounced publicly that a mother, distracted by children, would never be good enough to make an Olympic team. Joan savored proving her wrong. Not only did she come back stronger from pregnancy to win the U.S. cross-country title in 1995, she went on to qualify for the Olympics the next year. At the Olympics, the media hailed her as the Comeback Mom.

Joan saw her running program for moms as a way to reach out to other women, to bring them out of their boxes. "It's like we all live in our separate little suburban squares," she says. "But if we can come out of those squares and join a bigger circle of people, it doesn't feel so heavy, lonely, and depressing."

Just before the start of the training program, Joan got a call at home from an eleventh woman, pleading to be added to the group.

Her name was Mimi O'Grady, a stay-at-home mom with two sons and a daughter. Then thirty-four, Mimi talked fast and laughed heartily. *"Please,"* she told Joan like a child asking for another cookie, "I really want to join your group."

"Tell me why," Joan asked.

"Because I used to be a track star," Mimi blurted.

Joan was silent. "Where did you run in college?"

"I didn't," Mimi said.

Silence. "What kind of mileage do you do?"

"None," Mimi explained without a trace of irony. "I haven't run in seventeen years."

"Is she for real?" Joan thought to herself.

"Listen," Mimi went on to say, "I'm a track star . . . in my own mind."

Joan had to smile at Mimi's moxie.

The real story: Mimi had been a good runner in high school, good enough to qualify for the state cross-country championship. But she never went anywhere with her running. She didn't run in college, or out of college, or during her mommy years. Even so, Mimi was convinced she could be good again.

Mimi got a slot. She certainly fit Joan's target group in one sense: She felt holed up at home. She and her husband had recently moved from Pennsylvania to North Carolina. "I had no job and a baby on my hip," Mimi recalls. "I didn't dig in very quickly. The only friend I had was my next-door neighbor."

Joan called her new group "seejanerun," after the Dick and Jane reading textbooks from her childhood. She shortened it to just "The Janes." The women met Mondays and Wednesdays for ninety minutes, during that golden window of free time after young ones were dropped off at preschool.

Joan's goal from the start was to turn every woman into "a runner for life," no matter what her level at the start. That first season, they set a goal of running a 5K race at the end of twelve weeks. It would be a first for most of them. Running aside, Joan also wanted to give the mothers a chance to connect on another level. Before workouts, she would gather everyone in a circle like any coach trying to motivate her team. But instead of talking track, she would toss out a thought for the day for the women to think about. It could be a passage from Emerson or a musing from *Oprah*, lyrics from a favorite song or something from the morning's headlines. One of Joan's favorites was a quote from Thoreau: "If one advances confidently in the direction of his dreams and endeavors to lead a life which he has imagined, he will meet a success unexpected in common hours."

That was Mimi.

Among the recruits that first season, Mimi was the high-strung filly. "I was out of control," she admits. "All I wanted was to run really, really hard." Not accustomed to such full-throttle effort, her body couldn't yet match her zeal. During those first sessions, Mimi would gun it so hard she would collapse right onto the track. "I felt terrible," Mimi says, "but I felt free." She was happy to be off on her own for an hour or so without ever hearing the word "Mommy."

Joan mapped out individual training programs to build speed, strength, and endurance. She didn't coddle the women. She made them run intervals at different tempos. She had them sprint up a steep hill again and again and again. She timed them in the mile and guided them on long trail runs.

With her trained eye, Joan could see Mimi had raw talent, as well as something else. "She had a motor in her that no one else had, this gut strength," Joan says. The first time Joan timed Mimi in the mile, she clocked six minutes, twenty seconds. "Not bad," thought Joan.

By October—month two for "The Janes"—Mimi's mile time had dropped to 5:45. Around this time, Mimi ran her first 5K in decades and came in tenth with a time of twenty minutes, twenty seconds. In December, she ran another, this time finishing third for women with a time of 19:08, a little over a six-minute pace and back to her high school form.

In the car before practice one day, Joan told Mimi she really could have been a track star. "If I had coached you in college, you could have been an All-American," Joan said. "I'll coach you and train you now."

"But," Joan went on, "how does it feel to hear that now at your age?"

Maybe Joan expected to hear disappointment in Mimi's voice, or regret over what could have been, might have been, if only . . . But Mimi didn't miss a beat. "Guess my time is now," she announced to her friend.

This was what Joan was beginning to appreciate about all "The Janes." They had something she didn't always see in young, elite runners—gratitude. They weren't running to get scholarships. They weren't desperate to land a shoe contract. They weren't competing to please their coaches. They were running for the sheer joy of it—grateful just to be out of the house, among interesting friends, running along a shaded trail, or sprinting down a track as fast as they could. Of her friend, Joan says, "She knew nothing and everything at the same time. She was a prodigy who saw the race as its own reward. It took me twenty years to learn that."

"The Janes" helped Joan, too, in an unexpected way. Truth be told, Joan didn't have many friends who were moms like herself. Sure, she had colleagues in the track world, but these were mostly other competitors or coaches. Being around "The Janes"—new moms and veterans of all ages with dozens of kids among them— she found that she needed them as much as they needed her. In long runs or after workouts, she would learn things from these other mothers, the kind of intuitive knowledge that comes from experience and passes from one woman to another, from grand-mother to mother, mother to daughter. How to stay calm when a newborn is crying and a toddler is whining for more, more, more? How to function without sleep? How not to lose yourself to the unending needs of others? How to find time alone with your hus-band? "I had worked for twenty years to be a great runner," Joan says. "I wanted to work equally hard to be a great mother."

Joan became as much a pupil as a teacher. "She needed to know how to hang in there with three kids," Mimi says. "And I needed to learn how to run. That's truly what happened."

"The Janes" was so successful that first season that Joan held another session in the spring. Word had spread in Chapel Hill so Joan opened the group to twenty women for the second training session. She had to keep a waiting list. "The Janes" wasn't for every-one. Some thought the group was too intense. But for the women who returned season after season, it filled a hole in their lives. Four years into "The Janes," Joan sent out an e-mail as an April Fool's joke telling the group that a stay-at-home dad was interested in joining them. The backlash was instantaneous and fierce. One mom threatened to quit, while another warned that the group would never be the same. A third lamented the end of peeing in the woods.

As a regular, Mimi had improved so much that she got good enough to be one of Joan's training partners. Running side by side, Mimi, a brunette, and Joan, a blonde, looked like twin daughters of different mothers. Joan still had the competitive fire in her. At forty-one, she set a world record in the mile for her age group with a time of 4 minutes, 53.91 seconds.

Joan and Mimi became true friends, bonded by so many shared hours in the confessional of long runs. One weekend, after making child-care arrangements, they set off on a long trail run. A lean man their age caught up to them. After saying hello, he launched into his story. A father of seven, he was training for an ultramarathon—this was the second of two long runs of the weekend. Joan recalled that he laced his comments with words like "healthy" and "heroic." Joan did a quiet calculation in her head: two long runs, maybe four hours of road time, recovery naps in between. When did this man spend time with his seven kids? Joan didn't look at Mimi. Mimi didn't have to say anything to Joan. Their thoughts were braided. They knew just what they had to do. For the final miles, they picked up the pace. Fast, real fast. They started yammering about mundane things, making sure their breathing was as effortless as their conversation. Ultradad was having a hard time keeping up. He could barely spit out a word. After that, they never saw him again. And who said moms weren't macho?

The faster Mimi got, the more it fueled her drive to be better. But after a year, she hit a wall. Her times didn't improve. Worse, she started slipping. Her mile time slowed to five minutes, twenty seconds. Mimi could not figure it out. All she knew was that during practice it sometimes felt like a weight was sitting on her chest during hard runs. Once at the track, during time trials for the mile, she ran five minutes, thirty seconds and was so winded that she found herself veering in and out of her lane. A new member of the group, a nurse, asked her after a workout, "What do you take for your asthma?"

Mimi was perplexed. "Asthma?"

The diagnosis was dead-on. Mimi started taking medication for her exercise-induced condition and, once again, her times improved. Now able to push herself more, she trained for her first half marathon in Philadelphia. Mimi's race was as perfect as hitting and holding a high note in choir. She finished in one hour, twenty-seven minutes—just over a six-and-a-half-minute pace. "It was a thrill, not some far-off dream," Mimi says.

Nine months after the Philadelphia race, Mimi had another thrill: the arrival of a fourth child, another son. She trained with "The Janes" through most of her pregnancy, albeit at a much gentler pace. Even before the baby was born, Mimi plotted her return with Joan. She pledged to be back in her running shoes a month after the baby was born to pick up where she left off. This wasn't an obsession, Mimi made clear. It was something more fundamental. "Running," Mimi explains, "makes me happier."

Joan is the godmother of Mimi's baby, just as Mimi is the godmother of Joan's youngest daughter. "One thing I do know, Mimi and I will be running together when we're eighty-five," Joan says. "I wanted to be a great coach and what I got instead were friends, sisters for life."

CHAPTER 2

IRVINE

The Flying Nun

Sister Marion Irvine cuts a strong, striking figure at age seventy-five—five feet nine, hair as white as clouds, eyes electric blue.

And running shoes on her feet.

Her faith and her conviction that her remarkable running career was part of a larger plan is equally clear and strong. "I absolutely believe it was a gift from God," explains Sister Marion.

Indeed, her transformation seems miraculous: from an overweight desk-bound smoker in 1978 to an Olympic hopeful six years later at age fifty-four, twice the age of champion Joan Benoit.

There was nothing mysterious about her call to running: It came in the nagging voice of Jill Irvine, her nephew's wife. She bugged forty-eight-year-old Marion about getting into shape. Jill had started running to lose weight after giving birth to twin girls, her third and fourth children. Jill was soon hooked and she set out to convert Sister Marion.

"Even though she was twenty years my junior, Jill was my best girlfriend. She was really the closest I ever had to a sister," says Sister Marion. "But that didn't mean I was going to listen to her."

Sister Marion resisted. Later that spring, during an eight-day retreat at a convent in San Rafael, California, she needed a break. "It was very, very hot and it was getting hot in the chapel. I had to get away from the convent for a break. I had cabin fever so I thought maybe this is the time to get out and try this thing we're all supposed to be doing for our health," she says. She set out onto the street planning to run one mile down and another mile back. "It turned out more like fifteen steps before I had to walk."

But later, in the shower, she had a revelation. "I remember thinking I felt like an athlete. I suddenly had the resolve that I could go out and do better tomorrow.

"That resolve," she says, "is the hallmark of an athlete."

By the end of the retreat Sister Marion was doing the two-mile distance, walking half and running half. She kept it up after the retreat and six weeks later went to visit Jill and her family in Eureka on the Northern California coast. Jill was training for her first marathon and was going to do a long run the next morning. Sister Marion agreed to run the first mile with her, then turn and run back to the house. "I was really affected by what she was putting out in this sport."

The two ran out the first mile; before long Jill took off and Sister Marion was left with only her resolve. "That was the moment of truth. I could get back to the house any way I wanted. No one would know. But I ran. After that, I never ran anything shorter than two miles," says Sister Marion.

Unlike most beginning runners, Sister Marion did not extend her distance gradually beyond two miles in the typical run-walk pattern. "I don't know why, but instinctively I decided to stay at two miles until I could really run it fast," she says.

Four months later, she was running two miles at an impressive, seven-minute pace. It was all so easy. "I had a tremendous gift that

I didn't know I had. Any number of women my age could go out and do what I did but wouldn't get the results I did," she says. "But at the time I didn't know that."

Her next goal was to circle Lake Merced near her parents' home in San Francisco. By the end of the summer she had quit smoking and was watching what she ate. She began to enter 5K and 10K races.

In May 1979, Jill ran her first marathon, the Avenue of the Giants race, through the California redwoods. Sister Marion agreed to meet Jill under a bridge then run twenty kilometers with her. "It was raining sheets. I was huddled under my poncho watching the runners come. They kept coming but there was no Jill. I kept searching until I finally realized that I had missed her," says Sister Marion. Marion peeled off her slicker and raced four miles out when she saw Jill coming back toward her on the loop. "She was barely hanging on, but I stayed with her and she finished. It was really more like we were walking. Out there on that run I said, 'Next year I'll run it with Jill.'"

The next year both Jill and Sister Marion ran the Avenue of the Giants Marathon. After struggling so hard to finish the year before, Jill placed herself near the back of the pack. Not Sister Marion. "I wanted to win the thing," she recalls proudly. "I stood up front with the men."

To Sister Marion this was perfectly acceptable behavior for a nun. "God expects us to develop all of our gifts. I think that to go out and win a race gives praise to the Creator. I don't think winning is a bad thing," she reasons. At age fifty, Sister Marion finished her first marathon in 3:01. "I didn't know if that was good. I had nothing to compare it to. But people came up to me and said that was good and I could be a great marathon runner."

She began to run four marathons a year and in 1982 signed on with a coach who tried to teach her to temper her full-out runs. She improved, although the two had their battles. "If I had wanted to take orders from a man," she says, "I would have gotten married."

In 1983, she ran the California International Marathon and beat the time to qualify for the trials for the first women's Olympic Marathon in 1984. At fifty-four, she was the oldest woman to qualify for the trials. Her record still holds today. The trials were in Olympia, Washington. And Sister Marion says that those trials will always be the best. "There's never anything like the first," she says. The runners stayed in their own village on a college campus and ate special meals. They had massages and parties. "Everything you could possibly think of," says Sister Marion. "And it never occurred again. It was the bridal event."

At the trials she finished in the middle of the pack at 2:52. She remembers thinking that except for one forty-two-year-old, she was old enough to be the mother or grandmother of all the other runners. The winner, Joan Benoit, went on to win the Olympic Gold Medal.

Sister Marion figures her timing as a competitive runner was divine. If she had started any younger, there would have been no women's marathon trials. Four years later, she would have been that much older and the competition too strong. And if she had somehow discovered her gift in her twenties, when she was living the sheltered life of a young nun wearing a full habit, her interest would probably have just died away. She quips that the Vatican II Council, with its liberalizing of the Roman Catholic Church, made her running career possible. "I had changed, and the times had changed," she says.

After the Olympic Trials Sister Marion ran on the Master's circuit where she became famous in running circles as The Flying Nun. For a time she got interested in running track and competed in an international meet in Rome. "Long-distance runners like to hang loose and have fun. The people in track are trying to push you out of the way. It's dog-eat-dog. I loved it."

For several years Nike sponsored her with shoes and clothes and paid for her travel to races around the country and Europe. Before the race she would give a lecture on running and spirituality. "I started to be a roadie," says Sister Marion.

Through those years Sister Marion began to feel that spirituality was like running. You had to train for it. "I am spiritual and religious. Some people are not religious. But everybody is spiritual. It's up to us to develop that part that is our own essence," she says. Sister Marion has felt God's presence while running, especially on long sunrise runs along the Oregon coast when her footprints were the only mark in the sand. "You realize how small you are in the plan of things. It is humbling to be out there along the surf and the sand."

When she enters a large church, Sister Marion now tends to feel alone. "When I'm running I feel in harmony with the whole human family. I'm sure I've had my purest prayer, my best communications with God, while running."

Most of the time, though, her mind goes blank. During these periods, she feels she is generating spiritual energy, as if her legs were spinning turbines in her soul. "I feel as if I am putting this energy in a bank to use later," she says.

Then, in 1991, as abruptly as her competitive running career began, it stopped. "I just woke up one day and I knew I had run my last race," says Sister Marion. She had ignored hip problems and other injuries too long. After all, she was getting older.

"When you are at a high level of competition it is all-consuming," she says. "It's at the top of your mind all day. You're thinking, When will I run? What will I eat? My commitment to my religious life and my professional life were out of synch at that time. There was a desire to get more balance back."

Sister Marion has entered another type of race—one for social justice. She works to find housing for the homeless, help battered women, and comfort people with AIDS. She is still in contact with Nike, though now it is to monitor complaints about the company's labor policies. At seventy-three, she completed her first fast. For two weeks she and a small group of other Dominicans fasted and held interfaith prayer services in front of the United Nations in New York hoping to convince world leaders to find an alternative to war with Iraq. Between prayer services, she went out walking around Manhattan. She walks with a slight hitch, but she still lifts weights and runs thirty-five miles a week, just for herself.

When she runs, she often prays. Sometimes she prays for big things, like peace. Mostly, though, she prays for people she knows: "People struggling with addiction or illness or grief."

She knows what it is to grieve. While training again for the Avenue of the Giants Marathon in 1982, Jill was running along a rural road when a car crossed over into her lane. Jill was struck and died instantly.

Sister Marion ran the marathon through the redwoods alone that year. "I cried the whole way."

The woman who killed Jill was drunk.

When she runs, Sister Marion prays for them both.

CHAPTER 3

TREWORGY

Paving the way for her daughter

Up in the stands for a race, or watching unnoticed at practice, Cheryl Treworgy sometimes shakes her head in awe as she watches her daughter run. "She runs pure," Cheryl says. "She engulfs you in what she's doing. She takes you along." This is not just a proud mother talking. Cheryl is an athlete, too, who shares a passion for running with her daughter, Shalane Flanagan. Cheryl was a pioneer in distance running. A generation later, Shalane has grabbed everything the sport has to offer.

Shalane has collected NCAA titles, college records, and All-American status. She became a professional runner while still in college, made the U.S. Olympic team on her first try, and shuttles between meets in the United States and Europe. She has a coach, an agent, and a contract with Nike.

If Shalane is a symbol of all that women can achieve in running at the twenty-first century's turn, her mother is a reminder of just how hard it was to get there. As a high school student in the 1960s, Cheryl was banned from running alone at the high school track. *An unsupervised girl running laps? Never!* But mother and daughter shared a thirst not only to be fast, but faster: not only to win, but to win again and again.

Cheryl grew up a quiet, overweight teenager in Indianapolis. She can pinpoint the moment she decided to try running. It was while reading a newspaper story, written by the legendary coach Bill Bowerman, who espoused the health benefits of "jogging"—a word Cheryl had never heard. Bowerman, who cofounded Nike, said slow running was good for your heart and could help with weight loss. Cheryl laced up her Keds and went "jogging" in the park. "The weight came off," Cheryl said. "I was a runner."

At school, Cheryl would run laps around the track after she finished her practice as a majorette with the marching band. Running seemed to empower Cheryl, who had a difficult relationship with her stepfather. "It was my corner of the world where I was in charge," she says.

Once her jogging got up to a mile, Cheryl asked the coach of the boys' track team for advice. He gladly helped. Girls at North Central High School didn't have a track team. The closest Cheryl could get to the sport was keeping score at meets for boys. Itching to compete, she entered open meets at a local park and competitions through the Amateur Athletic Union (AAU), which attracted the same few teenage girls.

In 1963, running was such an oddity for girls that Cheryl had nothing to wear. She ordered boys' shoes by mail and had her grandmother make her shorts, which she paired with a mock turtleneck, a look positively Victorian next to today's belly-baring racers.

A tall teen at five feet eight, Cheryl was steered by coaches to longer events like the 800 meters. "Everyone was a sprinter," Cheryl says, "and I was terrible. I was just too big. I couldn't come out of the blocks fast enough."

Before her senior year of high school, Cheryl heard about cross-country—still a novelty for women in the mid-1960s. The idea appealed to her. Once or twice a week, she started running along the White River Parkway in Indianapolis. She loved it. That fall, Cheryl traveled to Massachusetts for the second AAU national cross-country championships. She finished seventh in her national debut. "That was all it took for me to realize, 'Hey, I might be good,'" Cheryl said.

Cheryl caught the attention of Indiana State University, which had a catch-all scholarship fund for talented students. She was awarded one—the first for a female athlete. Entering ISU in 1966 to study physical education, Cheryl was the entire women's track program. The men's team let her train with them. "They didn't cut me any slack," Cheryl recalls, "but I didn't ask for it either."

Cheryl had runners to practice with, but not runners to compete against. Fortunately, an ISU graduate student who was an assistant coach—and by her sophomore year, Cheryl's first husband—knew several high school cross-country coaches in the area and convinced them to let her compete with their teams—their boys' teams. Cheryl didn't mind, even when she had to give the boys a five-second head start so she didn't get in their way. But, as she proudly notes, "I never finished worse than third."

To race against women, Cheryl went to AAU meets, driving hours from Terre Haute to Chicago, Cleveland, or St. Louis. It wasn't until her final year that the university put together a women's "team," recruiting three other athletes from other sports. In 1969, ISU's inaugural women's track team competed in the first women's intercollegiate track championship in Texas. At the national meet, Cheryl won the half mile and mile, while anchoring the winning medley relay team. The others did well too. Amazingly, the ISU foursome tied for second overall.

At graduation, ISU's athletic department designated Cheryl an honorary "I-Man," recognition reserved for four-year varsity lettermen. While women's sports were still evolving at ISU, Cheryl felt nurtured rather than resented by her male peers. "I couldn't have asked for a better setting," she said. "They respected me because they saw how hard I worked."

After college, Cheryl and her husband moved to San Luis Obispo in California, where she taught physical education in middle school. She trained before and after a full day of teaching. More women were running, but one of the best was still in high school. Her name: Mary Decker. Cheryl couldn't wait for her to graduate and move up to the women's division at AAU meets. "She was fourteen, yet she was better than most of us," Cheryl said.

The world of sports was so lopsided along gender lines that after AAU meets, male runners from Cheryl's running club would shower and dress in locker rooms before the ride home. And Cheryl? She would find a restroom and stand over the sink to "shower." But at the college level, the tide was about to change dramatically. Congress passed a law in 1972 known as Title IX that had the effect of mandating equality in sports at colleges receiving federal funding. The "girls" would soon get their own locker room.

Cheryl was also too early for another trend: the wave of corporate money that was about to enrich the sport. Competing as an amateur, Cheryl was banned from accepting any endorsements or prize money. She trained alone on her own dime. Even when she made the U.S. team for the world championships—an accomplishment achieved five times in her career—she had to come up with her own travel funds. The most Cheryl ever got was two free pairs of shoes each year through her running club.

At twenty-three, juggling a full-time teaching job and marriage, Cheryl considered calling it quits. "I thought, 'Okay, it's time to start acting my age,'" Cheryl recalled. But if she was going to retire, she wanted to go out in style. And for that, she needed special coaching. Cheryl wrote a letter to one of the masters of the sport, Bill Dellinger at the University of Oregon, asking if he would coach her long distance via mail—the envelope-and-stamp variety. Dellinger's prodigy was the late Steve Prefontaine, the running world's idol. Dellinger replied: "I've never coached a girl before. Send me your times and I'll do a program."

He took her training up to sixty-five miles a week. Cheryl felt stronger than ever—so much so that she wrote to Dellinger asking what he thought of her doing a marathon. Cheryl had run a marathon the year before, mostly on a lark. She hadn't trained properly and walked the last six miles. This time, Cheryl was going to do it the right way. Not waiting for Dellinger's reply, she entered the 1971 Western Hemisphere Marathon in Culver City, California. There were a handful of women among a few hundred runners. She clicked along at a steady pace, ignoring the ex-Marine who tried repeatedly to run her off the road. She finished strongly in two hours, forty-nine minutes, forty seconds—a world record by almost six minutes.

When she called Dellinger with the news, he told her, "Glad you didn't get my letter. I didn't think you were in good-enough shape and said don't do it." News of her record rippled slowly through the running community. Although a growing sport, women's distance running was still a fringe activity. The AAU hadn't yet sanctioned the marathon as an approved event and, until 1972, the longest women's event in the Olympics was the 800 meters.

Even so, Cheryl's marathon record caught the attention of the producers of the television game show *To Tell the Truth*. They flew her to New York to appear. Celebrity panelists, the likes of Kitty Carlisle and Nipsey Russell, had to determine which of three women was the marathon record holder. The two decoys were models in sweat suits. "They were thin enough to be runners, but had no muscle definition," Cheryl sniffs. Most of the judges picked Cheryl. Her prize money went straight to the AAU.

By the late 1970s, Cheryl, who had moved around from coaching jobs at Oklahoma State and Michigan State, was ready to bow out from racing. Divorced, she had remarried, fittingly another elite distance runner, Steve Flanagan, a former stand-out miler from the University of Connecticut. The couple lived in Boulder, Colorado, where Cheryl was a buyer for a chain of running stores. Shalane was born in 1981, and a second daughter, Maggie, in 1983. Cheryl was recuperating from the birth of Maggie when Indiana State inducted her into its sports Hall of Fame. Her mother went in her place to accept the honor.

With their girls, Cheryl and Steve didn't push running. They kept their running stories and records to themselves. Shalane and Maggie grew up thinking it was natural for your mom and dad to go for a run every day. "Shalane would ask, 'When do I get to go?'" Cheryl recalled.

Then came a frightening scare. When her daughters were still very young, Cheryl was stricken with a heart condition. Her heart rate was out of control, reaching 275 beats a minute at its worst. Cheryl was placed on a life-saving drug that had debilitating side effects, including depression, fatigue, memory loss, and vision problems. It was a dark time. The couple, then living near Boston, divorced. Not until 1994 did Cheryl find a surgical solution to her problem. She underwent a seven-hour procedure that eliminated the rebel cells making her heart go haywire. It worked. Days later, Cheryl went out for a three-mile jog, ending a seven-year hiatus from her sport.

Shalane was a natural athlete, competing in swimming and soccer. She ran fast for a reason many girls—and her mother—would understand: She liked to outrun the boys in gym class. At Marblehead High School, Shalane was the girl to beat, winning three state cross-country titles, two outdoor track titles, and one national title in the indoor mile.

In her senior year, Shalane wrote a twenty-page English paper on the history of Title IX. She interviewed her mother, who recounted her war stories, including the time the school board barred her from running alone on the high school track. "That to me is just mind-blowing," Shalane says. "She had no support system. You had to be very driven because there were no tangible rewards."

For Shalane, however, the rewards were tangible. College recruiters came calling in her senior year with scholarship offers. On her short list were Villanova, Penn State, Providence, and her ultimate choice, the University of North Carolina. In UNC, Shalane picked a school that lavished both its women's and men's teams with services and top-quality facilities. The university had indoor and outdoor tracks, weight rooms, and physical therapy facilities. Athletes had access to trainers, doctors, a sports psychologist, and tutors.

Accepted at UNC, Shalane had a singular goal in college: She wanted to be a national champion. And she let it be known early on that if she was good enough, she would sideline herself in her senior year in order to train for the 2004 Olympics in Athens. Quickly, she became UNC's top runner, excelling in the Atlantic Coast Conference. A strong cross-country runner in high school, she became just as strong in track in college. In the fall of her junior year, Shalane won the NCAA Cross-Country Championship, held at Indiana State, her mother's alma mater. Cheryl, looking on with pride, was surprised when some of the men she used to train with in college came out to support her daughter as well.

The next year, while still in school, Shalane turned professional. Around UNC's campus in Chapel Hill, Shalane, with her white-blonde hair and chiseled features, was noticed. Young girls would recognize her on the street the way Tar Heel basketball stars were hailed in public. She had determination, to be sure. But onlookers at the track were impressed even more by her style—fluid, strong, graceful, fast.

Pure.

In the summer of 2004, Shalane qualified for the Olympic Trials with the fifth best time in the 5,000 meters. On the night of the final race, the stadium at Sacramento State University was packed. Her mother was trackside, taking race photographs for an online business she had started a few years before.

Shalane had a reputation for a slow kick at the end of the race. If she was going to win, she had to make all the others run her type of race. Cheryl was nervous, as always. "My problem is that I know too much," Cheryl said. "I know all the things that could happen." The first lap was slow, too slow for Shalane. She squeezed into the lead and set a pace about six seconds a lap faster, forcing the others to stretch. Now came the hard part: holding on until the end. With her hair tied up high with a ribbon, Shalane looked smaller and younger than the others as she led them single file. Her mother zoomed in with her camera for close-ups, showing the trancelike focus in her daughter's eyes. After nine laps with only one to go, Marla Runyan, older than Shalane by a dozen years, overtook her, only to be passed herself by veteran Shayne Culpepper.

With those two breaking away, Shalane was running scared, afraid that someone would nip her at the finish line for the third and final Olympic berth. A little sloppy for the last fifty meters, she

crossed the finish line three seconds ahead of her nearest chal-
lenger. Her arms and neck glistening with sweat, Shalane gasped,
"How did I do that?"

Her mother knew. And in Athens, she would see Shalane as an
Olympian, accomplishing a dream for both of them.

CHAPTER 4

WOMEN'S 5K CLASSIC

It takes a committee

The committee members slide into their swivel chairs around the massive conference table at the Alvin H. Butz Construction Co. in Allentown, Pennsylvania. Before them are the minutes from last month's meeting.

Item Eleven: Marilyn modeled the ear warmers and they are extremely cute!!

Item Fifteen: A beautiful quilt will be raffled among the breast cancer survivors.

Item Sixteen: The Red Robin Restaurant is on board to serve potato soup. The group decided that pierogis were not necessary.

The dozen women seated around the table—thirteen if you count two-week-old baby Lily—are not here to discuss construction. They have come, as they do on the third Monday of every month, to plan the long list of tasks that go into staging the annual Allentown Women's 5K Classic. "The Event," as committee members call it, is a women's-only race that has drawn up to 3,400 runners and walkers, including 270 cancer survivors, to Pennsylvania's Lehigh Valley.

Wendy Body, senior project manager at the construction firm and chairperson of the 5K Classic, has news. "I am so proud of myself. I got toilets for forty-eight dollars each. That's a savings of thirty dollars per toilet. That's a thousand dollars."

Held each October in a wooded valley along a branch of the Lehigh River, the Allentown Women's 5K Classic raises more than $100,000 to benefit local charities helping women with breast and other female cancers.

The largest women's race in Pennsylvania and the nineteenth largest in the nation, "The Event" is unapologetically girly. A pink balloon arch billows over the starting line. Men in tuxedos with pink cummerbunds escort the racers on bicycles. Finishers are rewarded with pink carnations, cookies, and champagne. The pages of its Web site are pink, with a flowery font.

Wendy and most of the women on the committee are serious racers who have trained hard and run with men at hundreds of races. This one, they keep for themselves.

"There are a zillion races every weekend that men will do," says Wendy. "We want this to be a place where women can try their first race in a nonthreatening environment. There's something very special about that. We have kept this race a protected environment."

Planning for the elaborate event begins two days after the last race ends. Over the years, the committee members have created bonds that go far beyond the pink blazers they wear on race day.

"If you look at these twelve women who meet every month through the entire year, we're constantly in contact, but we're all very different," says Jane George, who heads up the public relations subcommittee. "Some have grown children, some have brand-new kids. Some are married. Some are divorced. They're in all phases of life, but we're like sisters. I know I can depend on any of these women. But day to day, I'm sure our paths would never have crossed."

The race is now just six weeks away, and Wendy can't locate the huge finish-line banner that lists the names of the sponsors who have chipped in at least $2,000 to support the race. She calls over to the Lehigh Valley Road Runners clubhouse to see if it's there.

Other committee members have their own concerns.

"Are twenty-five hundred cups enough?" asks Annemarie Werley of the food subcommittee.

Jane Serues, who heads up race-day logistics, wonders if there is some kind of pink ribbon that can be used around the trailer for the timing equipment instead of yellow caution tape. "That just makes it look like a crime scene."

The volunteer committee reports that eighty girls from a nearby college have offered to help out at the race to earn service credits. "What?" asks Wendy. "Tell them to run the race."

Another volunteer hopeful writes: "I am a responsible ten-year-old girl. Put me where needed."

"Awwwwwwwwwwwwwww," is the response from the conference table.

Wendy takes a call from the clubhouse. No banner. This isn't the first year the banner has disappeared in the postrace mayhem. The committee has no warehouse of its own and volunteers gather up equipment and store it at their homes from year to year. "I don't have time to look for it this week," Wendy decides.

At times, off-point chatter erupts from subsections of the conference table. Lily is an irresistible distraction.

"Focus. Focus," Wendy pleads.

She insists on keeping the meetings to one hour. In addition to the minutes, Wendy has distributed a spreadsheet listing all 132 tasks that must be completed before the race. Each task has a committee member's name attached.

The most tasks—thirty-seven—are followed by the name Wendy.

Now in her early forties, Wendy's bouncy chestnut ponytail and apple-cheek smile belie her no-nonsense approach to getting things done.

"Wendy's amazing. She has such a cutesy way that you have no idea how capable she is—an engineer handling three or four multi-million-dollar projects at a time," says Jane Serues.

Wendy's mother Judy recalls an early commitment to community-service work: "She's the one who would skip the school dance to work on her Key Club project."

Wendy has run twelve marathons and participated in forty-five triathlons, including the Ironman at Lake Placid in 2003. Running, she says, is the secret to getting everything done.

"Being a runner definitely helps, mostly with the stress level of trying to maintain a pretty demanding job while working on an event that really has grown to the level where it requires a staff," she says. "Over seventy-five percent of the committee are runners and we discuss a lot of race details while out on the roads. It is a great way to have a meeting. I am so grumpy if I do not run."

As the meeting winds down, Wendy serves up pumpkin pie and hands out special shirts for the members of the committee that she paid for out of her own pocket. "We're getting to the point where we're all a little bitchy at one another, so I got them a surprise."

Each year, Wendy can count on at least one disaster.

One year, at 4 P.M. on the day before the race, Wendy learned the water company that was to deliver four thousand bottles of water had the wrong date.

"No matter how well prepared you are that last week will shock you," says Wendy. "That's when you need to be a crisis manager."

She had a friend who knew the plant manager at another water company. The plant manager agreed to sell the water, but the committee had to cart it out of the plant. Wendy's friend operated the forklift and hauled the water bottles out in the same rental truck delivering the race T-shirts. Volunteers unloaded the bottles by hand. "We couldn't exactly go to the store and buy four thousand bottles of water," says Wendy.

"The Event" was founded in 1993 when Wendy and some other members of the Lehigh Valley Road Runners Club decided to find a way to introduce women to running and help local charities. The year before, Wendy had participated in the all-female Danskin Triathalon.

"I came back to the Lehigh Valley all charged up about the thrill of standing in a crowd of almost one thousand women who were so fit. I distinctly remember watching a sixty-five-year-old woman running down to the podium to get her award and the feeling of complete awe. I wanted to capture the spirit of the women and bring it back to the valley."

The tenor of the committee was forever changed when an early member, Sandy Christman, in her twenties, was diagnosed with breast cancer. She died in 1999.

"I think Sandy really woke us up that breast cancer can attack vibrant and strong women," says Wendy. "I still cannot believe Sandy died, because she was such a fighter and had such a positive attitude."

Marilyn Taylor, who heads up the amenities and awards subcommittee, was diagnosed with breast cancer in 1989, and serves as a voice for the cancer survivor on the committee. She has handed out pink pens, pink gloves, pink caps, pink visors, and pink windbreakers to survivors who have crossed the finish line. Marilyn says the race has become something of a celebration for survivors and many of them host brunches for one another afterward.

"There was one girl who came and she'd had breast cancer in the summer but she was the kind of person who didn't want to tell anybody. She hardly told anybody, even people at work. She just took time off," says Marilyn. "When she came to "The Event" it was like her coming-out day."

While the health expo and the emphasis on helping women with cancer have grown, Wendy remains committed to the race's original intent—to get women fit. Each year several hundred beginning walkers and runners participate in First Strides classes preparing them for October.

"As long as I'm involved I will never lose sight of our first mission, which is fitness," says Wendy. "That affects a lot more women than breast cancer does."

At 7 A.M. on race day, heavy dew has settled on the valley. The parking committee is outlining parking spaces with lime. The food tent is humming with coffee and bagels for the volunteers. Crates of oranges and bananas are lined up. Mountains of race T-shirts have been folded and stacked.

"It's always fun to see the shirt. That weekend every other woman you see around has the shirt on," says Jane George.

A rumble comes over the hill with the arrival of the Lehigh Valley chapter of the Harley H.O.G.s, which provides security and traffic control, in full black leather and bandanas. "Us H.O.G.s want some of those pink blazers," says Walt Henne, president of the local H.O.G. chapter.

The roar of the Harleys fades as another sound builds. Hundreds of women are now streaming into the valley, gabbing as they go. One bunch is wearing pink bunny ears. Workers from the local Kraft

Foods plant carry a company banner. Many are wearing T-shirts with a photo of a mother or sister or aunt who died of cancer.

Finally, the pageantry begins.

If silencing the twleve-member committee is a challenge, Wendy must now hush several thousand women. "Okay, okay. I would like you to stop talking a moment. This is important to me," she commands into a microphone on the stage.

Laurie Flynn, a forty-one-year-old breast cancer survivor, takes the stage with her three young daughters. "I was bald last year. I was still facing chemo and radiation," she tells the crowd. "If you are diagnosed you can put up a pretty good fight if you're in shape." She went on to finish the race in 24:14, the fastest breast cancer survivor.

Compared to a typical weekend 5K, "The Event" is over the top. It's emotional. It's almost overwhelming. Among the thousands of charged-up runners whooping it up, many are blinking back tears.

Next comes an aerobic warm-up to the *Hawaii Five-0* theme. Wendy stands by the side of the stage shaking a pair of hot-pink plastic pom-poms. Finally, committee member Ingrid Berger sings the national anthem. When she hits the phrase—*"Bombs bursting in air"*—white doves are released from either side of the stage.

When the anthem is over, the racers flow toward the starting line and charge off along the river under willow trees, past a historic stone barn and over an iron bridge. A small boy on the stage cries into the microphone: "Go, Mommy."

And as the racers come over the finish, there above their heads is the once-lost sponsor banner.

Where was it?

Wendy smiles, and says: "After I yelled at about five people, 'How could you lose that huge banner?,' I realized it was in my basement."

CHAPTER 5

Cinnamon
SPEAR

On the faded trail of Chief Dull Knife

A bitter night wind raked over the young Cheyenne runners, gathered in a half circle on a remote Nebraska ranch. Everyone had their jackets zipped up and headbands pulled down low. They stood shoulder to shoulder, listening to the prayers of tribal leaders, who passed a sacred pipe of tobacco.

The runners had traveled to this place from their Montana homes hundreds of miles away for an open-air history lesson. The land here knew things—acts of selfless bravery, moments of unspeakable horror. More than a century ago, about three dozen Cheyenne—warriors, old men and women, mothers, children, even a baby—tried to escape the U.S. Cavalry by hiding in a creek-side hollow, where the ground had washed out. But they were cornered. Soldiers shot them at point-blank range. The rancher who owns the land now swears that at night, he hears voices rising from the ground—children talking and laughing, the murmurs of women, screams.

The Northern Cheyenne people named this place the Last Hole. As they prayed that night, one of the runners, eighteen-year-old Cinnamon Spear, took in the scene before her. "Look at us," she thought, "wearing gloves and stocking caps, Nike shoes and Columbia jackets, thinking *this* is hard. Just think of how our ancestors were. They were out in this kind of freezing weather for fourteen days and here we stand for less than thirty minutes."

At dawn the next day, Cinnamon and the others further traced the footsteps of their ancestors, embarking on a five-day, four-state, four-hundred-mile relay run. They ran through wind-whipped mountain passes, down icy roads, through snow squalls and subzero nights. They were trying to understand. The relay commemorated one of the most painful events in the history of the tribe—the thwarted 1879 escape of 149 Cheyenne from Fort Robinson in Nebraska. But "commemorate" is too weak a word. They wanted to feel the land, see the sky, and hear the wind. But they could never taste the fear of that time.

The Northern Cheyenne were skilled warriors who helped to defeat Lieutenant Colonel George Armstrong Custer at the Battle of Little Bighorn. They paid a price. Intent on subduing the Cheyenne, the U.S. government relocated them from the high plains of Montana to Indian Territory in what is now Oklahoma. The Northern Cheyenne fell ill in great numbers, dying of measles and malaria. They were unaccustomed to the hot climate; they lacked food. Two Cheyenne chiefs made a decision that would change their tribe's history: They would lead their people home. Chief Little Wolf made it to Montana, but Chief Dull Knife was intercepted in Nebraska by the cavalry. Confined to Fort Robinson, the tribe was ordered back to Oklahoma. Dull Knife refused. In a test of wills, the commander of Fort Robinson cut off food, water, and heat.

After five days, a defiant Dull Knife plotted a nighttime escape on January 9, 1879. Cheyenne warriors shattered barrack windows, allowing the others—mostly old people, women and children—to scamper into the darkness. Most were captured or killed on the spot. Some got as far as the Last Hole, only to be shot later. Dull Knife, his wife, son, and a few others escaped to safety, surviving weeks in the frozen wilderness by eating bark and the soles of their moccasins. They hid with the Lakota before returning to their homeland in Montana Territory, an odyssey that would be handed down in the tribe's oral history as "the long running fight."

The starting point for the current-day Fort Robinson Breakout Run is a rebuilt, log barrack, now part of a state museum. Runners are blessed with cedar smoke before taking off into the cold with great whoops and hollers. That's when it all clicks, recalls Ronnette Burns, twenty, a former high school cross-country runner. Sprinting into the morning cold, she pictured the Cheyenne mothers fleeing across the parade grounds of the fort, heading for the icy banks of Soldier Creek in moccasins and with blankets over their shoulders.

"It was easy to imagine that night," Ronnette says, "how they must have looked at the landscape, thinking how hard it would be to escape across the open space, the creek, the hill beyond."

The idea for the Fort Robinson Breakout Run was born of frustration. "Our traditional way of life was on the chopping block," explains Phillip Whiteman Jr., a forty-seven-year-old keeper of tribal traditions. "We were losing our language, our youth."

Phillip is an accomplished grass dancer, as well as an expert horse trainer and rodeo champion, who teaches young people on the reservation cowboy skills like barrel racing. He grew up in a home steeped in traditional Cheyenne ways. The first language he spoke as a child was Cheyenne.

Phillip was troubled by what he saw on the reservation. "Too many Cheyenne," he thought, "know little about their history." Even worse was the way so many succumbed to the hopeless escape of alcohol and drugs, discarding their tribal customs for hip-hop chic.

It came to a head for him in 1993 when the Smithsonian Institution returned to the Northern Cheyenne nation the remains of eighteen victims from the Last Hole massacre in Nebraska. Army surgeons in 1879 had removed the skulls of some of the Last Hole victims to research the impact of close-range gunshots. The repatriation of the remains 114 years later should have been an event of deep significance to everyone on the reservation. But Phillip claims most people knew the Fort Robinson Breakout only as a holiday each January.

Phillip, however, saw it as defining moment, a trauma that scarred the tribe for generations. After the breakout in 1879, public sympathy turned in the tribe's favor. Illustrated magazines and newspapers of the day, including the *Chicago Sun-Times*, exposed the atrocities. By an executive order in 1884, the tribe was given almost a half million acres in southeastern Montana for a reservation—an area of billowing, golden prairies and rugged hills studded with ponderosa pines.

This was the lesson that Phillip wanted to teach the others. "If we forget, their flight for survival will have been in vain," Phillip says. In 1996, he decided to organize a relay run within the boundaries of the reservation to commemorate the Fort Robinson Breakout. He set a time and place on January 9.

No one showed up.

Phillip had to cajole his middle-aged sisters and other relatives into joining him. About six of them took turns running seventy-nine miles, stopping at the reservation's four main towns. The next year was only slightly better. About twenty members of the tribe joined the run. By the third year, students got involved, lifting the number to almost one hundred runners. Then Phillip got a crazy idea: Instead of confining the run to the reservation, why not retrace the journey from Fort Robinson, four hundred miles to the southeast? And if that wasn't radical enough, he wanted to continue doing the run in January. He got thirteen recruits—including five juvenile delinquents, whom tribal leaders agreed to release temporarily from detention. Those were just the type of youth that Phillip wanted—tough, dead-end kids. That first year of the four-hundred-mile relay, many of the roads through the South Dakota hills were clogged with snow. With no money or sponsors, the runners had to sleep in vans. But the idea worked. "It was like a spiritual awakening," Phillip says. "It was a rebirth of their dignity."

There was another run the next year, and many more after that for an important reason: The Cheyenne grandmothers wanted it. They too often were the ones raising grandchildren for parents unable or incapable of doing it themselves. "The grandmothers were the ones who wanted their grandchildren to reconnect with their culture," Phillip says. "They came out in support, the people with troubled youth."

With each successful Breakout Run, the number of runners grew. Phillip brought the story of the relay into classrooms and recruited good runners. One of them was Cinnamon Spear.

All she knew about the Fort Robinson Breakout of 1879 was what she learned in her Tribal History–Tribal Government class at school. "I have to admit, by my senior year, I had forgotten most dates and names of incidents," says Cinnamon.

She ran everything on her high school track team—sprints, 3,200 meters, and even hurdles. Fair with blonde hair to below her waist, Cinnamon got her name when her mother thought the peach-fuzz on her newborn head looked the shade of cinnamon.

Although of mixed blood, her Cheyenne roots and ties to the reservation reach back generations.

The year of her relay run—2005—about ninety runners had signed up, ranging from as young as six to as old as sixty-five. Over the course of five days, they ran in rotation, with each vanload of runners taking turns running in pairs.

As she climbed into the front row of her van for the first leg of the journey, Cinnamon could see a bald eagle, peering down at the group from the branch of a big tree by a bridge near Fort Robinson. On the ride down from the reservation, an adult had told the runners to be on the lookout for animals. "They could be our ancestors watching over us," he had told the teens. *"Whatever,"* Cinnamon thought.

But this eagle . . . "As our van came closer and closer, I was sure it would fly away," Cinnamon recalled. "But it didn't. It sat there and watched. Every van passed, then it flew away."

Climbing from the plains of Nebraska into the hills of South Dakota, the runners saw deer and elk; horses and dogs; hawks flying overhead. They seemed to run with them, following just like the man had said. "It happened, I saw it, I believed it," Cinnamon says.

With such a range of ages and abilities among runners, some days were slower than others. One such day, the group had fallen woefully behind schedule, with forty miles to go before the next rest stop and in the waning hours of light. Phillip sent the youngest and oldest runners ahead to the motel rest stop and designated a special team of "Strong Runners" to pick up the pace. He asked Cinnamon to be one of them. She was exhausted, but honored by the request.

Snow was falling and the temperature plunged to near zero as night approached. Cinnamon was paired with another runner, her nineteen-year-old cousin, Randall. Sitting in the van with a dozen others, waiting for her rotation, Cinnamon stared out the window. Up ahead, she saw that the lead runner had stripped off his shirt.

"Why did he do that?" she asked.

"We started the day without our shirts," Randall told her, "and we're going to end it the same way."

When it was his turn to run with Cinnamon, Randall immediately took off his shirt. The idea caught on. One after another, all the boys started peeling off their layers to race bare-chested in the frigid air.

From the comfort of the warm van, Cinnamon wondered about running without a shirt. "What would it feel like?" she thought.

Hadn't they just learned about the women caught at the Last Hole, who had traveled for two weeks through the wilderness trying to elude the cavalry with only blankets to cover them? She wanted to know what they felt—to experience the numbing cold that would have engulfed those Cheyenne women so many decades ago. Silently, she started taking an inventory of all her layers. Sweater. Under sweater, shirt. Under shirt, long running bra.

"I'll do it," Cinnamon decided to herself. *"The next rotation, I'm taking it off."* In the van, she took off her sweater and shirt, her gloves and headband. She unbraided her hair and bolted from the van in only her running bra. "It was hard to breathe in the freezing air," Cinnamon says. "It was dark. I was afraid of slipping on ice or stepping on something and hurting my ankle, but that didn't slow me down. My hands were turning red. I was *soooo* cold. I only ran without a shirt, sweater, gloves, and headband for less than a quarter mile. What did I have to complain about? Nothing. It was nothing."

She got quickly back on the van feeling exhilarated. When the leaders decided to call it quits for the night, all the runners got out to run the final leg. In front was Ron, the first runner to take off his shirt. He held the tribe's sacred staff, tied at the top with eagle feathers. He passed it to Randall, Cinnamon's partner. The others began returning to the vans to warm up. In time, it was just Randall and Cinnamon, who kept one step behind Randall and the sacred staff as was the custom for Cheyenne women. Snowflakes swirled around them. "I couldn't feel my hands," Cinnamon recalled. "My face was stinging, my lungs hurt, but I wasn't thinking about any of that. All I could think about was how our ancestors had it way worse than we did. They were literally running for their lives and I was running for appreciation of my life. They gave the ultimate sacrifice for us today. And I gave that little personal sacrifice in gratitude of what they had done just for us to have a place here to call home."

At dawn the next morning, everyone gathered in a big circle. As part of the daily routine, Phillip and another elder went around the circle to bless each runner. Phillip then asked if anyone wanted to come to the center to address the group. Cinnamon was eager to speak. She wanted to tell the others—the ones who went back early to the motel—about the powerful feeling the runners shared the night before and how they, too, should try running without their shirts.

"I took off my shirt, let down my long black hair, and ran," she said. *Long black hair?* the others seemed to say with their faces. "I know I don't have long black hair, I know my skin's not brown, but that's how I see myself," Cinnamon continued. "It's not my fault I have blonde hair and it's not my fault I have light skin. It doesn't matter to me though because inside I see myself as a young Native woman. Regardless of how I look on the outside. Inside, my heart is Cheyenne."

This, after all, was the lesson of the Breakout Run.

CHAPTER 6

WINDSOR

Therapy in motion

On a cold day in February, when their daughter Meredith was just four months old, Bridgette Fahey's husband announced he just wasn't happy. He didn't know if he wanted to be married anymore.

He started staying out late and some nights he didn't come home at all. In April, after a big fight in the kitchen, he told Bridgette he was moving in with a friend from work.

"I fell apart. I felt it was all my fault," says Bridgette. "I would have done anything to make that marriage work."

For another year the couple waffled about the breakup. "I would say, 'We can make this work,' and he'd say no. Then he'd come back and say, 'Let's give it a try' and I'd say, 'Forget it,'" says Bridgette. "I didn't know from one day to the next whether I would be married or not. I was truly numb."

At twenty-eight, she was worried about how she would support herself and raise a baby on her own. She hired a divorce lawyer and began to see a therapist, but it was not until she entered another form of therapy that her future course became clear.

Bridgette had started running as a teenager and she continued to run into adulthood. She pushed Meredith in a jogging stroller, that first year after her husband walked out. The following January she saw an ad in a running newsletter for Team Windsor, a local women's running group that met near her home in suburban St. Louis. On a Tuesday morning, she came to a Team Windsor run with Meredith and the jogging stroller. Bridgette paired up with Judy West, the founder of Team Windsor, for a three-mile run.

"I think my husband's having an affair," Bridgette blurted out to Judy, moments after first meeting her. The Friday before Bridgette had seen an address on a document that indicated her husband was living at a different address than the one he had given her. "There was something that just didn't add up."

Bridgette spilled the whole story and Judy listened. The following day Bridgette confronted her husband and he admitted he was living with another woman. The friend from work turned out to be a girlfriend.

"That's when I knew the marriage was over," says Bridgette. "I didn't know a lot about myself, but I knew I wouldn't tolerate an affair. That was my line in the sand."

The next day, Bridgette found herself in a surreal situation. She met Team Windsor at the Chesterfield Mall for a run and was horrified to discover she would have to run right past the brown-stucco apartment complex where her husband was living.

Bridgette put her head down against the cold wind and ran past her husband's new address. "This is where he lives," Bridgette told Judy. "We were both kind of in shock. I couldn't believe I was able to run right past there."

Bridgette was on her way.

With Team Windsor, it's sometimes hard to know where the running club ends and the support group begins. It started in 1996 with a few neighbors. Every Monday night, as well as Tuesday and Thursday mornings, more than a hundred women meet to run or walk. They compete in local benefit races and in international marathons, the serious racers in blue-and-white sports bras and briefs, the walkers in baggy Team Windsor T-shirts.

From time to time, they declare a Ladies' Night Out and meet in a bar after the Monday night run to drink beer and eat chicken wings. On Halloween they run in costume. At Christmas they run through a drive-by outdoor light display.

But the team is not just an exercise group. It's therapy in motion. "When you're running, there is no eye contact. There's something about that that makes people feel safe. It allows them to let their guard down," Judy says.

GeAnn Powers, a club captain, adds, "You can go to Team Windsor with anything and people will be there to support you and help you work through problems. They let you cry on their shoulder and make you feel like you're not alone."

They were there for Nancy Maurer, when her multiple sclerosis took a turn for the worse and she could no longer drive because of her failing eyesight. GeAnn, who had suffered from postpartum depression and had a tendency to become reclusive, volunteered to drive Nancy to morning workouts.

They were there for Jael Lippert after her car was hit by a tractor-trailer, leaving her hanging upside down in her car for an hour until rescuers could free her. Team Windsor members took turns feeding her meals while she was bedridden in a full-body cast.

Judy knows that more serious runners may scoff at the women and their "team." But with their uniforms and coaches, the members push themselves to goals they might never have achieved on their own. Team Windsor even has a motto: *Life by Life. Mile by Mile. Dream by Dream.*

"If you look at a baseball team or a Cub Scout group they all have uniforms that define who they are," Judy reasoned. "Instead of us being a bunch of women running around aimlessly, we bond together as a team. We accomplish huge things, whether it is running a marathon or sitting in a divorce court."

The idea for the team started when Judy, who had been a champion runner at Bucknell University in central Pennsylvania, had her own dilemma. A former college teammate had asked her to run part of a 195-mile relay in Oregon. Judy wanted to do it, but she was used to training with a team. She had moved to St. Louis two years earlier for her husband's medical residency and was home with a baby. She had no team.

So she made one.

Her first recruit was Laurie Burke, who lived two doors from West in their subdivision, Pepper Tree Village. The two had walked together occasionally. Judy suspected Laurie, who was thirty-nine at the time, might have some untapped running talent.

"I will teach you how to run if you help me train for this," Judy assured her.

"Like a fool I said, 'Sure, I'll run with you,'" recalls Laurie, who was ten years older than Judy. "I had no idea she had a whole room full of trophies."

Soon Pepper Tree Village was up and running.

"First there was Robin, who said, 'Laurie's losing weight. I want to run,'" Laurie recalls. "Then it was, 'Robin's losing weight, I want to run.' Slowly the word got out that we were teaching middle-aged women to run."

Judy could rightfully call herself an elite runner. Among her many awards was an NCAA championship ring for coaching. Why bother with a group of ladies of marginal talent?

"It's not about me anymore," says Judy, whose own running performance had peaked several years before she started Team Windsor. "It is one thing to be able to win a national title. It is a totally different thing when you see a forty-two-year-old woman run her first mile and start bawling."

Many of the original members attended Windsor Crossing Community Church, so they took the name Team Windsor. The team does not charge dues, though from time to time a call goes out for funds to pay for mailings or to help a runner in trouble. On Halloween, Team Windsor members, in full costume, treat a low-income family with checks made out to the electric company. Judy is head coach of Team Windsor. There are also fourteen captains, who organize each run, two webmasters, an administrator and a speed coach.

"When I was in high school there were no competitive sports for girls," Laurie says. "I think for women my age that participation now gives us the sense that we're not just middle-aged nobodies."

Judy wanted Team Windsor to have the structure of a serious running team, but she didn't want it to get too serious.

"Most running groups have a competitive flair," Judy says. "I wanted to make sure it didn't matter if you were a thirteen-minute miler or a six-minute miler, you were still an athlete."

Captains go into every run knowing they may wind up strolling with a beginning walker, or jogging slowly with a woman working through a heartache. "Whenever you go out you have to be prepared to sacrifice your run to help another woman," Judy says.

With all that sharing in the air, Team Windsor could have become a prime breeding ground for gossip. But there is an unwritten code: "You don't take anything away from here and tell your neighbors. What is said here does not go back into the gossip circle," Judy says. In the early days there were some offenders. Judy says they "self-selected themselves out. They did not fit into the culture."

Bridgette embraced the culture and became a captain herself. "Team Windsor picked me up from one of the lowest points in my life," she says.

In her first year with Team Windsor, Bridgette ran every Tuesday and Thursday, with Meredith in the jogging stroller. But her daughter was starting to get heavy. Judy suggested Bridgette check into a local preschool so she could have a few mornings off. Bridgette had her doubts. She was afraid that if she sent Meredith to school two mornings a week it would look bad at her divorce trial. Besides, she couldn't afford it.

Judy insisted Bridgette at least take a tour of the school. "It was perfect for Meredith," says Bridgette. "I didn't know where I was going to get the money, but I figured it would come somehow."

She enrolled Meredith and on the first day she went to the office to write a check. The woman in the office started fumbling around and suddenly Judy walked into the office with two other Team Windsor runners. They were carrying a card signed by dozens of runners who had come up with $550 to pay Meredith's tuition for the year.

Judy showed up again when Bridgette was on her way to her attorney's office to give a deposition in her divorce case. As Bridgette was driving to the deposition, Judy called on her cell phone and demanded that Bridgette pull over right where she was. Judy met her in the parking lot of a garden center and followed Bridgette. As Judy sat outside the office and did paperwork, Bridgette gave her deposition.

A week later, Judy and four other women from Team Windsor sat silently in the back of the courtroom during her divorce trial. "I had a feeling she'd be there," says Bridgette. "I was afraid of the trial. When it came right down to it, I was afraid of my husband. He's six feet seven. I didn't want to make him mad."

Since then, Bridgette has responded to Judy's e-mails seeking help for other runners in need. "When Judy calls up the troops, you drop everything."

After the trial Bridgette still had her ups and down. "I had good days, but I also had days when I didn't stop crying." Her ex-husband moved to Washington, D.C., making Bridgette more or less a single mom. Bridgette went back to work part time as a nurse and made a life for herself and Meredith.

But Judy would have one more intervention.

Five years after her husband left her, Bridgette met a runner named John at a marathon training run. They saw each other in church from time to time and talked about their running injuries. Months later she ran into John at a party at Judy's.

"He's a really good guy," Judy told Bridgette, adding extra emphasis to the word "good." Two weeks later Bridgette ran into John again and another Team Windsor captain repeated Judy's "good guy" observation word for word. A few weeks later John sat next to Bridgette in church. When Bridgette reported that to Judy, once again Judy slowly repeated the words "good" and "guy." Bridgette got the message.

The next day she called John and asked if he'd want to meet for coffee, or a run. "I never would have done that before—only after being around all these empowered women," says Bridgette. "My whole confidence has changed. When I went into my marriage I was thinking, 'I can't let this guy go because there might not be anybody else.'"

Within a year, Bridgette and John were engaged and planning a spring wedding—a wedding that may come with its own race T-shirt.

"It's going to be small," says Bridgette, "but it would be very cool to have a 10K run."

CHAPTER 7

Darcy
GIBBS BATZOLD

Fighting cancer with her sisters

The Gibbs sisters were gathered around an indoor hotel pool, sitting on plastic chairs, sipping red wine from cups, swapping stories and laughs, keeping an eye on their daughters splashing in the water. Darcy Gibbs Batzold walked in, carrying a big cardboard box. She set it on the pool deck and opened it.

T-shirts. One for each sister, bright white, a little stiff, emblazoned with the logo of the 2002 Albany Race for the Cure, the 5K race they would run the next morning. The sisters would make their running debut in the race to celebrate Darcy's recovery.

Darcy, forty-five, pulled out one more shirt, this one neon pink for runners who were cancer survivors.

Darcy wrinkled her nose. "I'm not wearing it," she announced.

"What?!" shot back her younger sister Lauri. "You have to! After all you've been through?"

Darcy was adamant. She had her reasons. She felt good; she looked good. Her golden hair was thick again. Her body was fit and strong enough for her to run her first road race. Even at her new job, few people knew she had battled breast cancer. There was no reason to announce to everyone, *Here I am! Darcy the breast cancer survivor!*

Lauri, who had rallied the sisters to run the race, was crest-fallen. But Darcy argued that Albany wasn't that big a city. What if she bumped into clients or colleagues?

Faye, her closest sister, put a lid on the issue. "Darcy," she said, "you do what you want to do."

Darcy and her sisters didn't need a hot-pink shirt to remind them of her survivor's tale. When she was diagnosed with breast cancer, the odds were one in three that she would live more than five years. The day of the race marked four years, six months, and counting.

But Darcy understood cancer. Sometimes there were no clear victories, just reprieves. Maybe this was just a time-out. All she knew was that a few years ago she couldn't even walk to the next room without someone propping her up at the elbows. Now she could run for miles. "I need to do this for me," she says. "I need to know that after almost five years of hell, I can do what I used to do."

It had started during a bath. Darcy felt the tumor by chance; it was the size of a walnut. It stunned her: She'd gotten a clean bill of health after a mammogram just three months earlier.

Leigh, the youngest sister, went with her to the hospital on the day of her biopsy. The surgeon was direct. There wasn't just one tumor, there were three and her cancer was spreading fast. The sooner they removed the tumor and started treatment, the better. When they got home, Darcy went straight to bed. She looked at Leigh and told her, firmly, not to say a word to anyone. "I'll tell them when I want to tell them," Darcy instructed.

As soon as Leigh heard the bedroom door click, she went for the phone and began calling the sisters. No details, just the head-lines. *Lump in her breast. Aggressive cancer.*

One by one each sister called to talk directly to Darcy. "Now do you understand, Leigh?" Darcy snapped after taking yet another phone call. "I don't want this sympathy!"

There were six sisters, two brothers. Darcy was the tomboy. She tagged along with their father to construction work sites. She helped him install a swimming pool and dug holes for new trees. She was tough in mind and mouth, subtle as a sledgehammer.

But cancer terrified her. She was frightened for her daughters, then three and seven, and angry that of all her sisters, she was the first to face this disease.

Her whole life, Darcy had secretly envied each of her sisters. Jeannie, the oldest, was the strong third parent. Cindy was the softer sister—"Angel," her sisters teased. Faye was a triple threat: pretty, thin, confident. And Lauri and Leigh, the younger two, were everything Darcy was not. "They were different than me and my older sisters," Darcy recalls. "They had more freedom, more friends. When they would ask me to go out to dinner or bars, they were *it*! Everyone would ask them to dance. They were pretty and I was just this plain person."

Darcy was so entranced by her younger sisters that she started taking better care of herself. She started to run, hoping her size twelve body would melt to a size eight. She looked forward to the solitude of her regular three-mile run. "It cleansed me," Darcy said.

She kept up her running after the birth of her daughters. She loved long runs in the woods near her home in upstate New York. When her daughters were little, her husband would lift them into the back of his pickup, saying, "Let's go find Mom." And as they passed her on the side of the road, the girls would hang over the sides, yelling, "Come on, Mom! Come on!"

"I started caring about myself," Darcy says. "I wasn't happy in my marriage and I wanted to give this my best shot. As I started to run, it was such a refreshing feeling. I'd wake up in the morning, scoot out the door, run, and get ready for work."

When Darcy learned she had cancer, her marriage was already heading for divorce. The onset of her illness just sealed things. "I knew he was angry because our lives were going in different directions, but it gave me strength to fight," Darcy explains.

Darcy turned to "the girls," her sisters, and told them, "This is something I can't do on my own. I have two children and this cancer doesn't stop their lives."

The sisters swung into action. Leigh shuttled Darcy back and forth to the hospital. Faye coordinated schedules for the kids and sisters. Cindy cooked Darcy her favorite foods. Lauri entertained the girls. And all the sisters did what comes naturally: "Every time I started feeling sorry for myself, they'd give me a kick in the butt," Darcy says.

Her sisters made her laugh, too. When her hair started to fall out in clumps in the shower, Darcy called Lauri in a panic. Lauri, a hair stylist, came running with her clippers. Faye came running with a bottle of vodka. Lauri's advice: "Shave it off before you lose it." Lauri enlisted Darcy's daughters, Amber and Amanda, to help with shaving. The little girls put on dancing costumes and spun around. Lauri even got them to have a game of tic-tack-toe—on Darcy's head.

In quick succession, Darcy had a mastectomy, chemotherapy, and radiation treatment. But her cancer was so aggressive that the normal levels of chemo were not enough. To enable her to endure even higher doses, she qualified for a risky stem cell transplant at a Boston hospital. But the dangers were great: She had a fifty-fifty chance of dying from an infection because her immune system would be weakened.

Darcy was forced to broach a subject no one had dared to discuss: What would happen if she died? "I'd say to them, 'Sisters, if something does happen, you guys better get here and better spend time with my daughters and take care of them.' They were angry that I brought it up, but I knew they were all huddled in the corner talking about it anyway."

She didn't need to fear. "I knew if I ever decided to give up, my children would be okay because my sisters were there."

On the night she left for the twenty-four-day procedure, her sisters saw her off. As Darcy got in the car with Leigh, she paused to hug Faye. "We really didn't know if that was the last hug and for once we didn't know what to say," Darcy recalls. "When any of us gets upset or hugs or cries, we don't look at each other. But pulling away from Faye, her eyes met mine. We both blinked."

Isolated in her sterile hospital room, Darcy ached for her daughters. Faye solved that problem by arranging to have video-conference equipment set up in Darcy's room. The first time Darcy used it, she sat far back in her bed with a baseball cap on her bald head. She didn't want her girls to see how sick she looked. Often she had to abruptly hang up so her kids didn't see her vomit. The mega-doses of chemo were brutal. "You're literally on the toilet with a bucket to your mouth," Darcy recalled. "You feel like you just don't care and wonder how much more you can take."

Then, at night, Darcy would talk to her girls via the video hookup. "No matter what I went through during the day I knew in the evening I was going to see my girls. I looked forward to it and couldn't shut my eyes at night until I talked to them."

Seven months after she found the lump in her breast, Darcy came home—bald, thin, weak, and ghostly pale. Faye thought she looked ninety and feeble when she got out of the car. "But I felt like a million dollars," Darcy remembers. "I did it and there were my kids on the porch waiting for me."

After years of recovery, it was Darcy's oldest daughter, Amber, who planted the idea of her mom running again. Amber, a long-legged twelve-year-old, wanted Darcy to join her in a 5K race in Albany. Amanda, nine, also was planning to run. But Darcy didn't feel ready—physically or emotionally. "I was terribly afraid of failing," Darcy admitted.

Watching her daughters cross the finish line, Darcy thought, *"There's no reason I couldn't have run this race."* So when Amanda came home and said, 'Let's run in the Race for the Cure,' I was glad. I thought, *'Now's my chance.'"*

Darcy only spent six weeks getting ready for the race. Some evenings Amanda joined her at the track. Darcy realized her youngest was a natural. "I could barely get around one mile and she kept going and going," Darcy says proudly. "It's the same passion I had before I got sick. I remember how hungry I was for it."

Race day was a party for the Gibbs. Cindy and Lauri, the more experienced runners, outfitted Jeannie, a nonrunner who planned to walk, with her first running bra. Lauri, the fun, cool aunt, sprayed pink dye onto the ponytails of Amanda and Faye's daughter, Taylor, a seven-year-old hell-bent on finishing with the big girls.

At the starting line, Darcy and her sisters in their white shirts stretched as music blared and volunteers filled hundreds of pink balloons with helium. Among the thousands of runners, it was easy to spot the survivors in pink. Some ran with their heads wrapped in scarves. Some were strong enough only to walk. And some watched from the sidelines, their pale faces and sunken eyes bearing the tell-tale signs of a fight still under way.

And it hit Darcy: This business about the pink shirt wasn't

about her, a strong survivor. It was about the weaker ones on the sidelines, the ones who were ready to give up, the beaten women who Darcy sometimes would try to bolster with big talk about tenacity and mental strength.

With just minutes to go, no one noticed when Darcy slipped away. The sisters snapped photos of one another and waited excitedly.

Runners, take your mark . . .

Darcy hurried to rejoin the group at the start. Without saying a word to anyone, she had switched out of her white shirt.

To pink.

CHAPTER 8

WAITZ

The accidental legend

Jack Waitz really wanted to see New York. The Norwegian newspaper accountant had never been there, or even to the United States. His ticket would be his wife, Grete.

The year was 1978 and twenty-five-year-old Grete Waitz, an international track star and high school teacher from Oslo, had been invited to compete in the New York City Marathon.

Grete, who was thinking of quitting track to focus on her teaching career, wanted to see New York too, but she was not so sure about the marathon. She had never run one. The farthest she had ever run was thirteen miles.

But Jack urged her to give the marathon a try. Grete resisted, Jack persisted. Grete caved, and Jack packed their bags, turning the trip into a second honeymoon. The night before the race, Grete and Jack splurged at a fine restaurant on shrimp cocktail, filet mignon, red wine, and ice cream.

For all her track experience, Grete had no idea what to expect from a marathon. "Before the race I wasn't nervous. I felt great," she recalls. "I was running right behind the other female runners until we reached the Fifty-nineth Street Bridge leading into Manhattan—sixteen miles past with ten more to go. I felt strong and confident at that point and took the lead. I was the first woman on First Avenue. I knew I was in first place at that point."

As the race stretched into Upper Manhattan, Grete began to run into trouble. "It was easy for about eighteen miles, then I really felt the difference between a marathon and the other things I had been doing."

Grete, with her trademark blonde pigtails flying, was frustrated because she didn't know how to convert the mile markers to meters. She didn't know where she was and her English was not good enough to ask. And when her quads started cramping, she tried to drink water, but wasn't practiced in the marathoner's art of drinking from a cup while running and spilled most of the water all over herself.

"But I was so far ahead of the second girl I won very easily," she says. Grete not only finished first, she completed the 26.2 miles faster than any other woman in the world with a new record of 2:32:30.

"I was in such pain. I really didn't train for it," Grete admits. She could think of only one person to blame. "I was so mad at my husband because he had talked me into it. After I won, I didn't want to talk to anybody."

Instead, Grete took off her running shoes and flung them at Jack. "Never, ever, am I going to do this again!" she sputtered in Norwegian.

Luckily for the sport, Grete was not a woman of her word. The following spring, Fred Lebow, president of the New York Road Runners Club and founder of the New York City Marathon, coaxed Grete back to New York to run the club's six-mile mini-marathon just for women.

"I thought that was nice and I did it because it was not a

marathon," Grete says. But on that trip, Lebow talked her into running the marathon again that fall.

This time Grete actually trained. Again, she won and set another world record, 2:27:33.

"Then I was kind of hooked on the marathon," Grete says. "That is the race that made me a marathon runner. It opened a whole new door for me that I didn't know existed and changed my whole running career."

She returned to New York in 1980. She finished first again. Ditto for 1982, 1983, 1984, 1985, 1986, and 1988.

In the history of the New York City Marathon, one of the largest and most prestigious marathons in the world, no woman has come close to matching the glory of Grete Waitz. Eleven times at the starting line, nine times the first woman to finish.

In between those wins, Grete won the first World Marathon Championship in 1983, five international cross-country championships, and the silver medal in the marathon at the 1984 Olympics. She is Norway's marathon queen, in a sporting event that only began to build in popularity for women in the 1980s.

As a girl in Oslo, Grete was a tomboy behind two older brothers. "I was the youngest so I was always trying to keep up."

Grete's parents tried to discourage her boyish ways, but when she was twelve, Grete joined a local track and field club. "By then I knew I had some talent in running," she says. "I did very well and that was an inspiration for me." She specialized in running short distances. Later, she moved into middle distances and represented Norway in the 1972 Olympics in Munich, where she was among the first women allowed to run 1,500 meters. In 1975, she began to compete in 3,000-meter races.

"In those days women couldn't really run the long distances," she says, "and there was no road racing."

By the time Grete took on New York, the sport was poised for change. After her win in 1978, Grete had to ask Lebow for $20 to take a cab to the airport. Three years later, however, the sport was growing and there was enough prize money on the circuit that Grete could quit her job as a high school social studies and language teacher to run professionally.

"I realized I could make more as a world-class runner than a world-class teacher," she says.

Even now, after all those miles Grete remembers every race. "I can remember the way I ran it, the way the weather was. All of the races have something that makes me remember them," she says.

Twice in New York, she was plagued with stomach problems, including one year when she suffered from acute diarrhea. "It was a very warm day and I drank too much and it upset my stomach," she says. "It's an embarrassing thing to be running with crap all over your legs." Worse, the following morning Bryant Gumbel asked her about it on the *Today* show.

Her most emotional marathon was in 1992, when she ran the entire distance with Lebow, who was in remission from brain cancer before his death in 1994. Lebow had never run the marathon he founded in 1970. Grete ran by his side for five and a half hours, finishing behind 4,767 women runners.

"Over the years we had become good friends," she says. "It was very emotional." It was also physically difficult for her to run that slow. "For me, it is hard to run against my natural stride."

In 1990, Grete finally did retire from racing and, in a way, has returned to teaching. She has written several books of tips for marathoners and makes regular appearances at races to encourage other runners.

"I have helped a lot of people, giving them advice and training programs for marathons," she says. "That's something I enjoy doing. It is so nice to let other people experience the feeling of running a marathon."

During her marathon reign, Grete continued to come to New York each spring to run in the women's mini-marathon. And when a statue of Grete was to be unveiled at Norway's national track and field stadium in Oslo in 1984, Grete suggested the event be marked with a women's-only 5K.

"The race was meant to be only that one time, but more than three thousand showed up and to me it was a sign that we needed a race for women not only at that time," says Grete, who continues to sponsor the annual race. "It is no longer an unusual sight to see a woman, old or young, thin or heavy, running on the sidewalks. That was not the case in 1984," says Grete. "The race today is more like a tradition. Many of our runners are coming every year. We have walkers, slow runners, and fast runners. I wanted all women to feel comfortable and not pressured to perform."

Back in New York, along with the Norwegian consulate, she sponsors Grete's Great Gallop, a half marathon through Central Park. The race is in October and many of those planning to run the New York Marathon use Grete's race as a warm-up.

As the sport has grown in popularity, it has become a little slower. And so has Grete. "We're all older and slower now," she says. "If you look at the statistics there are more people in the big marathons but what is interesting is that on average we are slower today than fifteen years ago."

For someone who was completely driven to become a world-class competitor, Grete has no contempt for those who more or less waddle their way through marathons. "I personally think it is just great that people want to do the training and put the effort into doing a marathon even if they are waddling," she says. "You see women and men out there who would not have run twenty years ago because there were not as many slow runners as there are today."

Grete still runs forty miles a week, but if she goes much over that she tends to get injured.

"I run to keep my heart beating," she says. "When I was competing and I wanted to be the best in the world, that motivation was so strong I never asked myself, 'Should I go out and run?' I just did it. Now my motivation is staying fit and healthy and that motivation should be even stronger, but it isn't. So now I feel like the rest of them. If it's raining and it's cold and windy, I say, 'Oh, do I really want to go out today?' I can relate to all the excuses people have."

As much as she is identified with the marathon, Grete says there is one thing she would change about it. "I wish the marathon were fourteen miles," she says. "I think we all wish it was shorter."

CARROLL

The road to Hawaii

The vast lava field radiates heat like blacktop in the midday Hawaiian sun. It would be easy to quit, so easy. Theo Carroll has no energy left, she is sucking hot dry air, she is beaten. She could squeeze the brakes and get off the bike. Just stop. Her legs slowly turn the pedals, but she is drained. She will become a casualty of the Ironman Triathlon. That is clear. No shame in that, lots of people drop out.

Then Theo remembers the kids. Kids, heck—they're adults. And she's sixty-one. But they're her children, her kids, and they are waiting for her at the midpoint turnaround of the race, miles away. Another of her children, at home in Chicago, is tracking her progress online via a timing chip on her ankle, updating the ones on the ground by phone.

"I've got to push on," Theo thinks. "If my kids don't see me soon, they'll worry. They'll think I'm hurt." The mom in her kicks in.

She keeps grinding the pedals, pushing twice as hard against a twenty-five mph headwind to get half as far. Up ahead, Theo catches sight of a small group, waving signs. It's them. One of the signs says,

IRON MOM. Another simply, WE LOVE YOU. She approaches the turn-around and can barely make out what they are yelling. But the sight renews her.

"This is brutal," Theo tries to say as she turns around for the second half of the bike leg, another fifty-six miles of cycling, which is to be followed by a marathon run of twenty-six miles, 385 yards. Bernadette, the youngest at twenty-nine, turns to her siblings. "Did she just say, 'This is beautiful?'"

The uphill climb becomes a downhill coast. Resting her body and clearing her mind, Theo turns over a thought that has been with her all day. She is grateful her family is there to share this once-in-a-lifetime experience. But she can't help but wonder, "How could they be so forgiving of me, when I was so neglectful of them?"

Twenty years before, Theo Carroll was headed in a very different direction. Distant from her children, her husband, and herself, she was hurtling down a one-way street to self-inflicted ruin.

Binge eating had left Theo looking like a middle-aged beach ball. She packed 220 pounds onto a five-foot-two-inch frame. She inhaled two packs of cigarettes a day. And she drank too much, way too much. She'd start the day with a nip of vodka mixed with orange juice, then switch to beers and finish off a fifth of vodka by the day's end. To her daughter Bernadette, her mother was nothing but a source of endless embarrassment. "She was a fat drunk," Bernadette recalled with brutal clarity. "And I was never going to be like her."

This is not how Theo Carroll thought her life would turn out when she was a girl growing up in Michigan in the 1950s. A Girl Scout into high school, she had big plans. She dreamed of a future as a diplomat. She'd serve her country or maybe she'd join the Peace Corps. But at a party at Georgetown University her freshman year, someone offered her a beer. Turns out the shy Catholic girl from Detroit could become a good-time coed with an easy laugh. She went from straight A's to barely graduating.

Theo married just out of college and, at twenty-six, found herself with two young children and a husband in the Air Force. They bounced around a lot. "I was lonely," Theo explains. "There were not a lot of people to be friends with."

Two more children arrived. Theo loved her kids, but she secretly yearned for more. "On one level, I was a loving parent," Theo says. "But there was a real emptiness inside."

To fill the void, she drank. She'd have a vodka or two, or three or four. And when she drank, she ate. She loved salty, crunchy foods. Cans of nuts, chips and dips, cheese and crackers. These made the booze taste better. At night, though, she'd sit down for a proper meal with the family, pretending as if her day of binging on booze and food had never happened. It was her little secret. Or so she thought.

Her kids knew better. Bernadette coped by spending time with the friendly lady next door, a real mom. She didn't hide vodka bottles with the laundry. One day, Bernadette made a batch of chocolate chip cookies for her neighbor mom. After dropping them off, she returned home to find her mother seething with jealousy. Theo tore into her daughter. "Why would you do a stupid thing like that?" she screamed. "But, Mom," cried Bernadette, confused by the outburst, "I saved some for our family too."

Then there was the time Theo forgot to pick up her son Jamie from basketball practice. The nine-year-old started walking home but got lost. Three hours later, Theo found the shaken boy. Theo clearly remembers her oldest son, Nick, spitting out words that shame her to this day: *"Mom, I can't stand you when you're drunk!"* That was enough to send her into rehab. She made changes in her life. She got out of the house more. She helped at her kids' school. She went back to college, enrolling in a graduate program for counseling. For her first class, she wrote a paper about "controlled drinking," the idea that alcoholics can imbibe in moderation without returning to their drunken ways. Theo believed she could do that.

She couldn't.

Theo slid back to her old ways. Temptation was everywhere. Among the couple's circle of friends, drinking and eating were the glue holding everyone together. Pick a weekend, any weekend, and there'd be a party: thick steaks on the grill, spreads of sour-cream dip and bacon-wrapped finger foods, kegs of beer, and gin and tonics.

In 1986, Theo made yet another New Year's resolution to stop drinking, lose weight, and quit smoking—a triathlon of self-improvement. She was living near Tampa in an expensive, big house with her husband and two of their four children. After dinner one night, she asked her teenage son and husband to walk with her around the neighborhood. Theo rarely went out during the day for fear that neighbors would talk among themselves when they saw her waddling by in sweats that scarcely hid her fanny.

Theo cleared the dinner table and headed out the door. Her husband and son, lost in conversation, started to pull away from her. Theo tried to pick up the pace. Her thighs chafed with each step. She fell behind, panting. This wasn't running, it was walking. One foot in front of the other. And Theo couldn't do it. The others were a block away, then two blocks. Theo had to stop in disgust. "What have I done with my body that I can't even walk?"

In the summer of 1987, Theo and her husband planned a party to open a beach house that had belonged to Theo's aunt. The night before, as Theo got ready for the party, she knocked off a bottle of champagne. But why stop at one? She drained another. Her mother found the empty bottles. "Why couldn't you wait?" the older woman implored. Theo thought she could hide her habit. But she could no longer deny that everyone saw her as a drunk.

A month after her mother confronted her, on September 14, 1987, Theo Carroll took her last drink. It would be too much of a fairy tale to think that sheer willpower made Theo sober and fit. No, it was a year of grueling work. Theo started seeing a counselor to deal with her drinking, and the reasons for it. She had to admit that she felt hollow and trapped in her marriage. Now sober, she came to realize that all she had in common with her husband were their four children. Making matters worse was the boom-and-bust cycle of their finances. Their quality time revolved around partying with neighbors. Take that away and what did they have?

Only after Theo had controlled her drinking was she allowed to enter a drastic weight-loss program. Like many obese patients, she began with a strict protein-shake diet, five shakes a day for six months. After that, she had to count every calorie. In six months, she lost a hundred pounds.

Finally, she could move. She took walks on the beach. She started lifting weights at the gym, swimming, and taking aerobics classes. She bought a rowboat to use on a waterway near her beach house. She loved being out on the water at dawn under a salmon-pink sky. Dolphins would come right up to her boat. "I was alone with the world," Theo says.

In her fifties, Theo finally had the life she'd wanted as a teenager heading into the world. In 1993, she earned her doctorate in counseling from the University of South Florida—and the next day served her husband divorce papers. She moved out of the house and into the family's beach house. Her daughter Bernadette, just out of high school and battling her own dual demons of drugs and drinking, visited her mother on weekends. They talked for what seemed like the first time, filling a void of many years.

Theo had reinvented herself. She had a career as a therapist, specializing in eating disorders. She taught classes at the university. Instead of belonging to the party circuit, she belonged to a gym. She was a regular swimmer. So it was not unusual when a friend asked her to join a relay team for a local triathlon. "What's a triathlon?" Theo wanted to know.

It sounded fun, but Theo didn't think she was good enough to compete. She passed on her friend's offer. But when she later saw an ad in the paper for another local triathlon in the summer of 1997, she signed up. "I went out and just did it," Theo says. It was a mini-triathlon near Sarasota: a .5-mile swim, 14.2-mile bike ride, and a 3.1-mile run. "I fell in love with it," she says. "I couldn't believe I had finished. It was one of those 'Wow' experiences."

One wow led to another. Theo wasn't a stellar competitor, but neither was she the last one over the finish line. She kicked it up a notch, trying longer distances and cross-training. Some mornings she swam for an hour or two; others she ran. She logged miles on her bike on weekends. Running was her hardest event. She ran at a twelve-minute pace. As distances got longer, she followed the Jeff Galloway marathon method—choosing to run two minutes and walk one.

As a therapist and recovering alcoholic, Theo knew firsthand the grip of addiction. She kept her exercise in check, scheduling workouts with the help of triathlon trainers. She didn't obsess on her exercise or fret if she missed a day. Exercise became part of life, not all of it.

She was amazed how, with discipline, she could push her body to greater and greater limits. And as distances increased, so did Theo's ambition. The woman who couldn't walk around the block was now setting her sights on the Big Kahuna—a full Ironman with a 2.4-mile swim, 112-mile bike ride, and 26.2-mile run. For her birthday, Theo asked her kids to come with her to an Ironman competition. She had set her sights on a race in Florida, but on a lark, she put her name in the lottery for the championship in Hawaii, the biggest and most storied competition. To her amazement, she was one of two hundred lottery winners.

Bernadette, Anastasia, and Nick traveled with their mother to Kailua-Kona on the Big Island. So did Theo's best friend, Ramona. Only Jamie, in Chicago, couldn't make it.

Of 1,800 competitors in the Hawaii Ironman, only sixteen were women like Theo between the ages of sixty and sixty-five. The race started under the canopy of an orange dawn. The swim in crystal water over coral reefs was mesmerizing—a lull before the windswept bike ride that almost broke Theo's spirit. But by the time she hopped off her bike for the marathon leg, Theo was ahead of half the women in her age group.

Theo ran most of the marathon course in solitude by the light of the stars and moon. By mile six, she saw competitors who had already finished walking home with their bikes on their shoulders. She knew she would finish, trusting her walk-run routine to carry her the distance. With less than ten miles to go, Theo caught up to a woman her age who was close to her breaking point. "I don't think I'll finish," the woman told Theo dejectedly.

Theo coaxed her along. "This is how I'm going to do it," said Theo, explaining her run-walk strategy.

"Can I do it with you?" asked the woman, running and walking in tandem with Theo the rest of the way.

At the home stretch, spectators by the thousands jammed both sides of Ali'i Drive. Even though the winners had finished that afternoon, it seemed like everyone had returned to watch the final athletes drag themselves across the finish line. The place had the feel of a Mardi Gras party.

Theo and the other woman could see the finish line with the big digital clock. "Go on," Theo told her running mate. "You go first."

Theo felt the crowd's support lift her like a wave rolling to shore. After pushing herself all day, now joyous to the point of delirium, Theo looked remarkably calm, smiling widely as she clocked in at sixteen hours, twelve minutes and five seconds. In the crowd, in the glare of floodlights, she saw her children waiting for her. She fell into their embrace, hugging all of them and not letting go. Anastasia placed a purple lei around her neck. Bernadette, herself sober for three years, beamed with pride, and felt a surge of inspiration. "You're awesome," Bernadette gushed.

The Ironman medal that Theo was awarded was validation of her physical accomplishment. But Hawaii was so much more than that. She had her kids back.

FELT

Recovering from 9/11

It's now or never, thought Sandy Felt at the end of the summer of 2001. She was running five or six miles regularly. Her forty-fifth birthday was around the corner. She told her husband that if ever she was going to run a marathon, now was the time.

"If you want to do it and you dream it, you can do it," Ed Felt replied. "I'll be there at the end, scraping you off the ground if I have to."

Days later, Ed took off for a business trip on the West Coast, boarding United Flight 93 from Newark, New Jersey, to San Francisco.

It was September 11, 2001.

When hijackers took over the plane, Ed was able to get to the lavatory and call 911 on his cell phone before the plane crashed into a black pit in western Pennsylvania.

Left alone to raise two teenage daughters, Sandy was angry. She spent sleepless nights in Ed's basement gym, pounding the treadmill or swinging at the red leather punching bag. At just five feet and a hundred pounds, Sandy walloped away at the bag. For inspiration, she imagined the center of the bag was the face of the plane's lead hijacker, Ziad Samir Jarrah, who had never met her, or Ed, or their daughters.

For Sandy, who was always very private, grief has been solitary. She has friends and family, but she was extremely close to her husband. They became friends on the third day of freshman orientation at Colgate University and two years later began dating. That was it. They were together for the next twenty-five years.

"Running has been my way to grieve," says Sandy. "It's that constant friend that I have with me on bad days. I can put my sneakers on, and as hard as it is to get going I know that once I finish the run, I'm going to feel better. Even if I'm just lying to myself."

In the months after Ed died, Sandy continued to run, alone, on trails near her home in Matawan, New Jersey. "It was how I kept my sanity," she says.

But with so much running, her weight had dropped to just eighty pounds. Sandy had to force herself to eat so she could keep going.

In April 2002, Sandy went to a hotel in Princeton, New Jersey, to hear the cockpit voice recordings of Flight 93's final moments with others who had lost family on the plane. While she was there, Sandy met Elsa Strong, whose sister, Linda Gronlund, was a flight attendant on the plane. Elsa was organizing a group of family members to run in the upcoming New York Marathon to honor those who died. Sandy signed on.

"Something deep within me said: 'I think we can do it.' It's part of my healing process, but it is also a tribute to Ed's faith in me," says Sandy.

Ed, a computer scientist, never ran a marathon, but he regularly ran four or five miles. On Sundays, before church, he often took a twenty-two-mile bike ride. In the summer, he swam twenty laps at the neighborhood swim club.

"He believed in living. He explored a lot of things and enjoyed the challenge of living, not just existing," Sandy says. "He always pushed me that way. I had been the kind of person who sat back. I just kind of watched everybody. But this time I felt I needed to push myself out."

After committing to Elsa, Sandy trained all summer. By late summer her weight was back up. During a training run in August, she was strong enough to get away from an attacker who had parked his car along the busy road. As Sandy passed, the man grabbed her hips from behind.

"I elbowed him and he lost his grip on me. Then I ran like a bat out of hell," she says.

On another lone training run she realized her mind was strangely adrift. She tried to count backward in her head from one hundred and kept getting stuck at fifty-eight. She took out a mint and sucked on that until she remembered fifty-seven.

In October, less than two months before the marathon, she ran Grete Waitz's Great Gallop, a half marathon in Central Park. There she learned her body was in shape, but not her head.

When she got to the finish line, it struck her that Ed wasn't there. "I completely lost it," Sandy says. "I completely broke down. There was no way to prepare for that."

Fueled by sadness and anger she continued to train. By now, the marathon had come to mean much more than a foot race. "This grieving process has been a birthing process in so many ways," says Sandy. "These monsters killed my husband. I can't let them kill me, and my daughters. I have to continue living."

On the day of the marathon, the fifteen members of the Flight 93 team showed up in matching red shirts with an American flag on the front and the words: "Flight 93 Family Runners. They never gave up and neither will we."

Sandy set out on the course by herself. She wore a button with Ed's picture on her shirt.

Along the way, Elsa and some of the other family members stopped to be interviewed by reporters at prearranged spots. Sandy knew where those spots were and made sure she slipped past unnoticed.

"At that point my mind was focused on getting through this task," Sandy says. "I wasn't focusing on Ed and I wasn't focusing on being depressed."

After the half marathon in October, she went into the New York City Marathon with an iron determination that she would not let herself think about Ed: "I knew where not to go."

Only once did she struggle to keep him from her thoughts, as she ran through the quiet streets of the Hassidic section of Brooklyn. "You could hear your own footsteps. It was so eerily quiet. That was the only time that shook me up," Sandy says.

"The rest of it was music and dancing," she says. "You could smell all the different foods. It was making me hungry."

Around mile thirteen she was feeling good until she saw a man running next to her suddenly collapse. At that point, she decided she was not going to push it. She was there to finish.

By mile twenty she was struggling. Her brother-in-law met up with her there and told her that Elsa and another Flight 93 runner were coming up behind her. Sandy took off her jacket and waited. She would not finish alone after all.

"We decided to run together," she says. "We'd been talking to each other over the past six months. We thought it would be nice."

Sandy finished the marathon in five hours and forty minutes.

When she crossed the finish line, Sandy was cold. She couldn't find her sister-in-law, who had her clothes. She was hungry. Starving.

But she wasn't thinking about Ed.

"I kind of felt he was with me all along," she says. "I didn't focus on it. I remembered his words, and that he had faith in me. That was enough."

CHAPTER 11

Susan Marilyn
PAJER and DARROWS

The runner next door

Susan Pajer lived one door from Marilyn Darrows and always thought they would make good friends. They seemed to live parallel lives. Susan had remarried and was raising four sons: three from her first marriage and a two-year-old son with her second husband. She called the young one her little caboose. Marilyn, two years younger, was also on her second marriage. She had three older daughters and a sixteen-month-old caboose of her own. Susan was a serious runner who owned a running store in town with her husband. Marilyn taught aerobics at two health clubs.

But Susan and Marilyn had time only for friendly waves from their driveways and promises of, "We should get together someday." With teenagers, toddlers, husbands, households, and jobs— not to mention laundry, meals, car pools, orthodontist appointments, parent-teacher meetings, and dogs—who had time for new friends? They couldn't arrange play groups for their youngest kids, let alone coffee with each other.

Some mornings, Susan would see Marilyn running with her husband, Kim. He was fifty and lean. Gliding through the subdivision every day of the year, he was the neighborhood "runner." All of which made the news on that rainy day in the autumn of 1999, a bolt out of nowhere. Phone calls from house to house passed the shock from neighbor to neighbor. Did you hear about Marilyn's husband? Chest pains. Stress test. Gone. Right there on the tread-mill at the hospital. *Tsk, tsk.*

Susan wanted to reach out to Marilyn, everyone wanted to help, but how? What do you say to a woman who was married for less than three years and left to raise a toddler in diapers as well as teenagers? From her window, Susan could see the procession of peo-ple making their way to Marilyn's front door. Neighbors walked in carrying casserole dishes and left dabbing their eyes with tissues. Susan waited more than a month. She went into her youngest son's room and packed up some of his old clothes in a cardboard box— all of his unisex fleece tops and bottoms in primary colors. Not sure what she would say to Marilyn, she strode across the lawn that sep-arated their homes and rang the doorbell. Marilyn looked like a snarling dog, coiled and ready to pounce. She was in no mood for another well-meaning neighbor bearing food. She had entered a new phase of grieving: anger. She was sick of all the people looking at her with pleading eyes and asking, "How are you doing?"

"Not another one," Marilyn thought as she stared at Susan with a toxic mix of annoyance and impatience.

Susan held out the box. "I won't be needing these anymore," Susan stammered. "I thought you could use them." Quickly, she added, "We ought to go for a run."

Marilyn paused and thought, *"Thank God for this one. She doesn't want to wallow in my sadness. All she wants to do is go for a run."*

"Yes," Marilyn eagerly said. "Yes, I'd love to go running."

A few days later, Susan and Marilyn bundled up their little ones and tucked them into running strollers. Marilyn was an occasional runner, but she was fit from teaching aerobics. They looped around the subdivision. They made a date to meet every Tuesday morning after the older ones got on the school bus. And when it got too cold to run with the toddlers, Susan's husband, David, volunteered to watch them. He made the kids waffles in the shape of hearts and announced the launch of the "Tuesday Morning Breakfast Club."

Susan and Marilyn started with three-mile runs, building to six miles. Before Susan had shown up on Marilyn's doorstep, her doctor had wanted to put her on antidepressants. But running, she discovered, was just the antidote she needed. "I saved you thousands in therapy bills," Susan likes to remind her friend.

The women found things to talk about from the first mile.

"Doesn't life just suck sometimes," Susan tossed out one run as an opener. Marilyn wanted to scream and shout. *"Yes,"* she thought, *"this is a woman close to my own heart."*

They talked a lot about their kids. About husbands—first and second. About child support. About Marilyn's attempts at middle-aged dating. About life alone.

Susan was good at helping Marilyn to focus her energy, deciding what to fret about and what to let slip away. As time passed, Susan nudged her friend to think about dating again and helped her evaluate candidates. And she could commiserate about what it was like to go to "Back to School" night and feel as if you were the only single parent in a room full of happy couples. "We never, ever stopped talking when we ran," Marilyn said.

They jogged all over Doylestown, a quaint county seat near Philadelphia. To onlookers, they seemed a little like a Mutt-and-Jeff couple. Susan was blonde and willowy; Marilyn was brunette and pint-size. If it was raining or too cold to run, Susan and Marilyn would go down to Susan's basement and run on the treadmill, taking turns running and talking.

One morning after a long run, they trotted up to Susan's driveway only to find David with the car running and both kids buckled into their car seats. "We had a little accident," David explained calmly. Marilyn's daughter, Mikayla, had fallen and sliced her head. They raced to the pediatrician's office, still sweating and wearing their running bras and shorts. In an examining room, the nurse looked at them and asked, "Aren't you the ones we just saw running outside?"

Marilyn was thinking, *"Yes, that's me, the bad mother who left my child to go running."*

But all the nurse wanted to know was how they could run and talk, talk, talk all the time.

Marilyn got so good at running that she decided to join Susan in a local 5K race. As the owner of a popular running store—the Training Zone—Susan was a fixture on the local running circuit. She wasn't as competitive as she used to be, but she could hold her own at the front of the pack on any day. On race day, Marilyn was nervous and having second thoughts. "I kept thinking, I have no business being here with all these runners," she says.

But a funny thing happened on the way to the finish line: Marilyn beat Susan with an impressive kick in the final yards. She finished in twenty-four minutes. "She's got those little legs that she can turn over quickly," Susan said with pride about her friend.

As the years have passed, Susan and Marilyn have had to make some adjustments in their running schedule. They still try to run every week, but some mornings it's only a short three-mile jog before the kids are up. "We create the time for running," Marilyn said. "I've never found another sport that gives me the same lift. You can solve life's problems and you get a workout."

And on those days when Marilyn gets cranky and irritable, her daughters might gently suggest, "Mom, maybe you need a run?"

That would be all she'd need to hear. Reaching for the phone, she would call Susan. "Ready?"

The
NDEREBA SISTERS

Running for Kenya

Each morning, the sisters ran three miles to school along dirt roads, kicking up clouds of dust in the dry months and clods of mud during Kenya's rainy season. At lunch, it was three miles back to their village for lunch. Then back to school again and home when the day was done. Each way, they ran. Twelve miles a day, five days a week.

Catherine Ndereba was the oldest, a runner from childhood, a runner by necessity, who is now a runner known far beyond the hills of Kenya. "We didn't have a school bus or anything," says Catherine, who speaks swiftly, her English accented with an African rhythm. "We had to go to school by foot. So we ran."

And she continued to run, into adolescence, into adulthood, and into international stardom. Four times she has won the Boston Marathon, and she set a world record in Chicago only two years after running her first marathon.

Her sister Anastasia, two years younger, is also a professional runner, working a weekend circuit of marathons, half marathons, and 10K runs in the United States and Europe. Her dream is to run in the Olympics with her sister.

Catherine and Anastasia, who grew up with nine brothers and sisters on a farm where their father raised cabbage and carrots, are now among the world's elite Kenyan runners. They train in the United States, travel the world to international competitions, and are celebrities at home where they make appearances at ribbon cuttings and speak to school groups.

These sisters found a way out of Africa's rural poverty and a culture that offers little or no opportunity for women.

They ran their way out.

When they were in middle school, Catherine and Anastasia began to run in a network of local running clubs that stretch across Kenya the way Little League and travel soccer do in the United States. Catherine and Anastasia were on the Leopards. Their older sister, Caroline, was on the Elephants.

"We were in one club and we had to compete with each other to see who would be first and who would be second," Anastasia recalls. "People were cheering us and that is the time I became motivated to keep on running. Sometimes I defeated her, sometimes she defeated me, but we kept on running."

In high school, their coaches had Anastasia pace for Catherine. "When I paced for her no one would defeat her," says Anastasia.

Their father, Joseph, a talented runner who never made it up the rungs of competitive running in Kenya, encouraged them. "Whenever we could run at athletic meets he would work so hard to make sure we had enough pocket money to spend," Catherine recalls.

Catherine's schoolmates called her "Crazy Ndereba" because she would take off to go running on her own. "It was like it was in my blood. I couldn't spend a day without running."

After high school Catherine made the Kenyan national team and was hired by the Kenyan prison system. In Kenya, elite runners are offered good government jobs to help support their running careers. Anastasia, who was also a soccer player in high school, had suffered injuries, but after high school she moved in with her sister in Nairobi to train. "I chose my sister's same career and she kept on giving me encouragement," says Anastasia. "I was willing to defeat her, but I was not willing to remember that I had not been training and she had trained."

Anastasia ran with Catherine for several months until she suffered a knee injury that kept her from racing for a year. In 1999, she began to train again, but she'd gained weight. Catherine took her out for a run in the heat and made her wear a sweatshirt. "She wanted me to shed weight," says Anastasia, who struggled as the sisters ran a long loop together. "I was running and running and I told my sister, 'I don't want any more running. Let me go back.'"

Catherine pointed to a bus in the distance and asked Anastasia if she wanted to ride back. Anastasia sprinted to the bus, looking forward to a ride home. After she got there, she learned she had been set up. Catherine was not carrying any money to pay the fare. "When we got to that vehicle my sister said, 'I will not give you the fare. If you want to walk home, that's good.' So that is how she dealt with me. That was the time I felt like my sister hates me," says Anastasia.

"I knew she could do it," says Catherine, "but she didn't believe she could do it."

They continued running back to Catherine's house.

"I felt like dying," says Anastasia. "When I arrived in the house I entered into bed without taking off my clothes and I slept there. I didn't want to talk to my sister anymore."

That didn't last long.

"After all that, now I have seen the fruit and I have seen how she has helped me," says Anastasia. "You have to persist. You have to persevere. That is how my sister was showing me. I see that she taught me to go from one level to another."

Catherine had experienced tough runs, too. In 1998, she decided to ramp up her running career and left her one-year-old daughter with her husband in Kenya so she could train in the United States, where she could focus on her career and receive better coaching. The next year she ran her first marathon in Boston. She came in sixth and, exhausted, collapsed into a wheelchair at the end of the race.

She continued to train and won in Boston the next two years. In 2001, she set a world's record for the marathon in Chicago, completing the race in 2:18:47. She won again in Boston in 2004 and 2005. "Boston is like my home now," says Catherine, who has been nicknamed "Catherine the Great."

In 2003, after competing for several years in Europe, Anastasia followed her sister to the United States to train. For four to five months each year, the sisters live in a big home outside Philadelphia owned by their agent, Lisa Buster. There is room in the house for up to ten runners at a time. The Kenyans train nearby in Valley Forge National Historical Park, where George Washington and his ragtag troops wintered from 1777 to 1778. "It's so beautiful. It's quiet running there in the morning and seeing the deer jumping in the grass. It reminds me of home," says Catherine.

In their off-hours the runners cook spaghetti, rice, and ugali, a corn-meal mush that is a staple in Kenya. They watch TV and go to the mall. Catherine likes to shop at Macy's, Dress Barn, and Marshall's. A born-again Christian, she watches only the Christian Broadcasting Network.

A win in Boston earns $100,000, but many weekends Anastasia and the other lesser-known runners compete in small 10K races and half marathons for anywhere from several hundred to several thousand dollars in prize money. "This is my career. This is my job. I don't have any other job," says Anastasia.

When they are home in Kenya, Anastasia and Catherine often speak to young girls who are runners. "Sometimes young ladies drop out when they are like eighteen," says Anastasia. They become interested in men, she says, and other distractions. "You have to talk about how that's not good," she says. "You have to have your own principles as a lady so that you can make it. You have to have some discipline and self-control. If you do not have discipline, you cannot make it in life."

Catherine met her husband, Anthony Maina, when they were both working at the prisons. He takes a major role in raising their daughter, Jane, when Catherine is competing. While Catherine represents a new kind of Kenyan woman, together, she and Anthony and Jane represent a new kind of Kenyan family. "Women in Kenya are changing," says Catherine. "Some years before many didn't believe they would have a chance to go to school or do sports like we are doing. They only believed it was men who could do that, but now you can see that the women are doing it and nobody is discouraging them anymore."

Anastasia is now among those coming up behind Catherine. Over all these years, and so many miles, she has never been jealous of her older sister's success. "I have never ever felt that way," says Anastasia. "When I see her winning, I feel it is myself. When I see her cry, I cry too."

"My sister keeps on motivating me," she says. "She always tells me, 'You can make it. You can do it. Be strong even when the speed is too high.' When I cannot go farther, she keeps on telling me, 'Keep on going. You will make it.'"

OSLOSKY

From tragedy, a turning point

The old man in khaki shorts visits at the most unexpected moments. Sandy Oslosky might be putting on mascara or brushing her hair, when suddenly he appears in her head. Her hands turn cold. She clutches the counter for balance. "Please go away," she'll think. "Not now." But she can't escape. She knows where he will lead her—back to that misty summer morning, to a run by the beach, to a moment that changed her life.

The old man is walking in the opposite direction of Sandy on a bike path next to a busy road. Sandy jogs with her dog Princess on a leash. Her husband trails on a bicycle with their daughter on back in a seat. The family is out for their regular morning jaunt while on vacation at the shore in Delaware.

As the old man approaches, he gives Sandy a friendly nod and a "Good morning." Sandy nods back. In a blink, the man's smile contorts to a grimace. *"Look out, look out! Get out of the way!"*

Sandy pivots. She sees a black Pontiac Firebird careening off the road. The speeding car slams into her husband's bike, rolls over, and smacks into a road sign. Her daughter catapults into the air and lands in a lump. Her husband slides across the pavement under the bike, hitting Sandy and knocking her into a ditch.

She opens her eyes and feels the stab of panic. *They're dead, they're dead! How could they not be dead?!*

She hears crying. It's her nine-year-old, Alyssia. Sandy scrambles to her feet to look for her. The girl's bloody arm is so mangled it looks like it could snap off at the elbow with a tug. A few feet away, her husband stirs but cannot stand. Sandy cradles her daughter, who, to her relief, is more worried about her dog than her arm. "Where's Princess?" she implores through tears. "Please get Princess."

In minutes, the scream of sirens grows loud. Medics lift Alyssia onto a stretcher. Another team works on Sandy's husband, Andrew. At the hospital, doctors do the best they can, but Alyssia's injury is too severe for them to handle. Sandy, still in her running shorts and sports bra, gets in a helicopter with her daughter for the two-hour flight to the Children's Hospital in Washington, D.C.

As she prepares to leave, medics bring in a third patient—the twenty-three-year-old driver in handcuffs. Drunk, he had fallen asleep at the wheel. His injuries were nothing more than bruises.

"There he is, walking in virtually unscathed," recalls Sandy. "And I'm thinking, *'What's wrong with this picture?'* I just want to kick the shit out of him."

She walks up to the man and looks straight into his bloodshot eyes. "I'll pray for you," says Sandy, controlled but strong, "but you have to pray for my daughter."

The driver turns away.

It took months for Sandy's daughter and husband to heal. In many ways, it took Sandy even longer. "My daughter nearly lost her arm; my husband had several broken vertebrae," she says. "My injuries were all mental."

She was haunted by the crash and was lost in the legal system. Police charged the driver with reckless endangerment. But getting from Point A to Point B—from seeing the driver in handcuffs to hearing a judge's sentence of six months in jail—was a bewildering journey through a judicial forest, where Sandy could neither speak the language or decipher the way. "I kept asking the district attorney, 'What's the next step? What's the next step?' I didn't understand any of it," Sandy says. "I never fully understood what the lawyers were telling me. I'd hang up the phone after talking to the prosecutor feeling absolutely stupid."

One day, the prosecutor on the case called Sandy, inquiring about how the family wanted her to proceed. Were they going to hire an attorney to seek damages? "It was real difficult. I had my own questions, but had no clue how to ask them or what to expect," Sandy says. The lawyer was compassionate, but her very competence made Sandy feel that much more inadequate. She sulked. "Honey," her husband said, "why don't you go for a run? You'll feel better."

And she did. She put down the phone and headed out the door. She ran for three miles, five miles, eight miles, ten. She had taken up running more than five years before and knew she could pound out her problems in a good workout. Life took on a different perspective when she was running. It was not so much a runner's high as a runner's clarity. On that very run after talking to the prosecutor, Sandy suddenly knew what she had to do.

She would become a cop.

Just like that, it came to her. "I convinced myself to look into a criminal justice school and policing," Sandy remembers. "That way, I'd never feel like a total idiot again when I dealt with our justice system. And I'd be able to be out there and stop every drunk driver on the highway."

She didn't announce her plan. She didn't have to. She knew that if she believed she could do it, she would. It was a reflection of her new outlook on life that emerged a few years before the accident when she started to run. Her whole life, Sandy was a self-proclaimed slacker who took the path of least effort at every turn. No ambition, no determination. All of that changed with running.

Sandy had learned a lesson about running. It was not just about exercise. It was about testing yourself, setting a goal, trying for another, pushing for the next mile-mark, and savoring each accomplishment. Before the accident, in the span of more than five years, Sandy went from walking around the block with effort to finishing a marathon in less than four hours. To her astonishment, she was a natural. She started entering races—and winning her age group. It gave her confidence; it made her competitive. And she decided if that formula worked for running, why not apply it to the rest of her life?

"That's where it started," Sandy explains. "You're out there running and you see what you're truly capable of doing. You start to think, I can do that."

This resolve came as a surprise to Sandy. She was born and raised in Ligonier, a postcard-perfect little town in western Pennsylvania's fox-hunt country. Exercise was never part of her childhood. "I hated to sweat," she explains. Sandy was a high school senior when she started dabbling in all the things parents warn about. "Dumb and young" is how she describes her younger self. She got pregnant at eighteen and dropped out of school, just four months shy of graduation. She did what she thought was the right thing and married the father of her daughter. It didn't last long. "I was a poster child for every social dysfunction," she says.

Life improved. Sandy married again, had two more children, and ended up working as an office manager for her husband, a chiropractor. But she always hid the fact from her children and friends that she didn't have a high school diploma.

Sandy started running for a reason that would be familiar to many: a home video. There was no doubting the camera; she looked like a blob. She wasn't obese, just lumpy. "I didn't look like how I thought I looked," Sandy explains. She was in her thirties and knew it would be all downhill from there if she didn't start to exercise. "I started out just walking alone through Ligonier," Sandy says. "I set goals, saying, 'Well if I can walk this far, maybe I can add a little to it.'"

She began jogging, adding miles, then mapping out a four-mile loop in the hills around Ligonier. She picked up the pace of her running. She dropped fifteen pounds. When a neighbor suggested she run in a 5K for the local YMCA, Sandy reluctantly signed on—and finished second behind a woman a decade younger. "I started running every 5K I could get to," Sandy recalls. "I got bitten."

A 5K led to a 10K, which led to a half marathon, and finally the holy grail, a marathon. Sandy discovered not only was she good at running, she liked it. Her training runs were her time to think. She would rehearse conversations she needed to have with her kids or husband or coworkers. She'd recite the lyrics to favorite songs. She'd think about the day's headlines. "I can cure all the world's problems in a good three-hour run," Sandy explains. "Your mind's working. You can replay a problem over and over and work it out. And afterward, your problems don't seem quite so bad as before."

It was because of running that Sandy decided to go back to school, earning the equivalent of a high school diploma. Decades of hiding the fact from everyone around her gave way to a desire to tackle her secret head-on. "All of a sudden, I'm out there winning races and enjoying it," Sandy recalls. "And I thought, if I could do that, why couldn't I face this demon and put it to rest?"

In 1998, before her accident, she began training for her first marathon with two neighbors, Ann and Patty. They ran together every week. On one training run, they made a twenty-mile uphill trek over the Laurel Mountains from Ligonier to Johnstown. Run that hard and that long with someone, you learn things. Runners talk about the high they get from running. For Sandy, running was a dose of truth serum. She felt she could share anything with Ann and Patty.

"I don't want you to think poorly of me," Sandy began, midway into a run, "but I'm a dropout."

Her friends let her continue, their legs beating out the same tempo, all eyes ahead. "I'm tired of being embarrassed about it. I'm going to get my GED," Sandy told them. "It was a crappy decision to drop out of high school. I never wanted to admit it, not to you, not to my kids."

Sandy could feel her shame melting like ice. "All right," enthused Ann, sensing her friend's unease. "Let's have a party to celebrate! It'll be a graduation party— sheet cake and all!"

Sandy needed that, just like she needed Ann and Patty to bolster her in training. In May, the friends finished the Pittsburgh Marathon. In June, Sandy earned her GED. And the next year, she watched a drunk driver nearly kill her husband and daughter.

After the accident, at forty, Sandy enrolled in a criminology program at Westmoreland Community College. Her decision to become a police officer was less about revenge than diffusing her anger. "I thought if I get an education, I can know what this legal system is all about and maybe go on to do something grand and noble," she explains.

Sandy surprised herself. The former dropout enjoyed school. Other than her struggles with math, she sailed through her courses. She got accepted into the police academy at Indiana University of Pennsylvania. She learned how to fire a gun and how to "take down" an unruly suspect. She took classes on search warrants, the court system, testifying, and writing citations. In physical tests, she more than held her own, setting an academy record in the women's mile-and-a-half run of ten minutes, three seconds. The academy named her the outstanding police cadet of the term.

The Ligonier Police Department hired Sandy as the town's first female officer. She started out part time, and at the same time kept up her studies, thanks to a scholarship. On campus, Sandy did her best to fit in. But she was painfully aware that there weren't many students with three children, a husband, and a mortgage.

Her first weeks on the Ligonier force, Sandy rode around with veteran officers to get a feel for things. She was working over Halloween weekend when a call came over the radio for a two-car accident. Possible DUI. A driver made a left turn into the path of an oncoming vehicle with two elderly women. Witnesses said the driver, a woman around fifty, immediately left the scene and ran into a tavern. "Great," thought Sandy. Here are two old ladies, sitting on the curb all shaken and bruised, and the culprit is probably knocking back beers and will say she only had a drink after the accident. Instead, Sandy found the driver scared and full of despair. She sobbed all the way to the hospital, where she had to have her blood tested for alcohol. "I'll never drink again," she kept telling Sandy. This was Sandy's first DUI as a cop—a moment she had anticipated and rehearsed for a long time. But there was no lecture from her. No guilt trip for the driver. No anger. Oddly, she felt empathy for this woman and offered her words of encouragement.

Only later, doing paperwork back at police headquarters, did the memories of the accident come flooding back. Now working full time as a cop, Sandy has discovered that every accident dredges up memories of that summer. But it no longer unnerves her like before. She knows how the story begins. And now, she has written an ending of her own, with her daughter providing the epilogue. Alyssia, the little girl on the bike, has turned into a star runner. She thrives on competition. At thirteen, she entered a popular 5K trail run near her home and beat out hundreds of older women and teens to finish first. As a freshman in high school, she ran on the varsity cross-country squad. Her mother cheers her every race. Often, onlookers will notice the big scar on Alyssia's arm and ask Sandy about it. "She was hit by a drunk driver," her mother will say. And if they press her for details, she'll return to that misty summer morning, to a run by the beach that rocked her world.

CHAPTER 14

Centipede
LADIES

The ultimate connection

Julie Rohloff snaps the bungee cord onto her nylon mesh belt. Noreen Searls snaps herself in, too. Then Jill, and Stephanie, and Wendy, and eight more runners, until the connection is complete. Each year, these thirteen women tie themselves together and run 7.4 miles uphill from the San Francisco Bay, through Golden Gate Park to the Pacific Ocean.

Individually they are marathoners and milers, wives and mothers, workers and students. Together, they are a centipede.

The centipede emerges each May to run in San Francisco's wacky Bay to Breakers race. Founded in 1912 to lift the city's spirits after the devastating 1906 earthquake and fire, the race is not unlike the city where it takes place—a goofy combination of mellow good cheer and flamboyant exhibitionism. Seventy thousand people run in the race, many of them in costume—everything from Elvis impersonators to Smurfs to a rolling Tiki bar. There are those who wear nothing at all.

Then there are the centipedes. Official race rules state that the thirteen members of a centipede must remain connected at all times and measure sixty feet in length. The lead runner is required to wear antennae on his or her head. The last runner must have a stinger attached to his or her rear.

"It's a race like no other," says Noreen, who with Julie is cocaptain of the centipede entered each year by the Aggies, a Northern California running club that, in its serious mode, routinely sends men and women to Olympic running trials.

The Aggies have dominated the women's centipede competition at Bay to Breakers since women first ran it in 1987, though in recent years the rival Bay-area Impalas have been challenging.

The club's official motto is, "The faster we run, the sooner the fun." Even the most competitive Aggies get into the spirit of this ultimate team race, says Julie. "Running is usually an individual sport. It can be so isolating. This is the one time, when you are literally tethered together, you are truly running as a team."

The teamwork shows right from the start of the race when the centipede sets off in a V-formation. The strongest women pull the others along by their waists.

"Sometimes we scoop up slower men in the V," says Julie. "We seem to attract a lot of naked men, but we don't even look."

Along the way there are some strategy discussions.

"If you race alone you can have your own strategy, but when you're tied to twelve people everyone has to have the same strategy," says Julie. "We have a captain up front and we talk about it. We try to decide if we should just push as hard as we can. We ask out loud, 'Are you okay? Are you okay?' all down the line. If you hear a yes, you push hard. If you don't hear anything, you look for water."

"You have to take care of the person in front of you and the person behind you," Julie says.

If the team is running well enough ahead of any challengers it will opt to make the famed Lenichi Turn in Lindley Meadows of

Golden Gate Park at the six-mile mark. The Lenichi Turn is a full 360-degree turn named for two entirely fictional eighteenth-century Eastern European centipede runners, Oscar and Igatoo Lenichi.

Yes, indeed. This is San Francisco.

In January, Julie calls the centipede squad to check if they're in shape or pregnant.

"That was always my spring excuse to get fit," says Noreen, who has run all but three of the races since 1990. She skipped once because she was finishing her college degree and twice due to pregnancy. "I've got a lot of T-shirts," she says.

There is a set of about ten regulars, but some years the Aggies need to invite new runners into the centipede.

"In the past this has been a very sensitive issue," says Julie. "One year a woman was really upset with me. She really wanted to do it because it looks like it's so much fun, but people don't realize how hard we're really running."

Julie has to be cautious when mixing five-minute milers with those who run a six-minute pace. The race captain, too, is selected with care. "We usually pick somebody that I know is aware of everybody's ability and is somewhat compassionate."

The winning centipede gets $500 from the race organizers, but the real reward is brunch, says Noreen. Bay to Breakers invites winners in each division to a championship brunch. "It's a very nice brunch and it's the one time a year that we can all get this big group of ladies together."

One runner comes from Idaho and another group comes up from central California to run with the Bay-area Aggies. "When we all get together we ask, 'How are your kids?' We talk a lot. We solve all the world's problems on the warm-up and the cool-down," says Julie.

The first Bay to Breakers centipede appeared in 1978, dreamed up by thirteen male runners from the University of California, Davis, on a road trip back from a track meet. They ran together with their heads popping up through a sheet of black, plastic weed-blocker.

"We showed up there and ran the race and had a lot of fun," says Julie's husband Dirk, a founding centipede runner. "The reception we got was overwhelming and the next thing you know, there's a centipede division the following year."

A core group of those runners went on to join the Aggies Running Club, which has won the men's centipede division all but four times since that first race.

In the 1980s, the club began to attract more women runners, and in 1987 Julie organized the first female centipede. "We decided, 'Hey, we can do that too.'"

The goal of the Aggies' male centipede is to finish ahead of the first woman runner, says Dirk. "It's a macho thing to beat the first elite woman. We did that for many years, but the women have gotten much faster and we have not done that in the past few years."

The goal of the female centipede, he taunts Julie, is to finish ahead of the first naked male runner.

No, she corrects, her centipede is focused on beating the male centipede from San Diego that runs the entire race wearing over-sized sombreros. "That's not so easy to do at a 6:15 pace."

There are other differences between the male and female centipede, says Julie. The men grunt. They swear. "When they pass somebody they say, 'Hey, we hammered him' or 'Get out of the way.' We would never do that."

For many years the Aggie women wore the traditional centipede costume that allowed only their heads to show above a swath of silky, parachute material that was printed with the logos of club sponsors including PowerBar, Microsoft and Reebok.

But in 2002 the Aggies, who now run wearing the Asics logo, had a disastrous race on rain-soaked streets.

"Someone in the back fell and we all went down," Julie recalls. "The lead woman ripped the costume and took off without us. She finally felt that we weren't there and turned around. We picked each other up and she waited until we caught up."

The Aggies tied the costume together to remain in compliance with centipede rules, but finished second behind the Impalas.

The following year they copied the bungee system from another centipede.

"Now we can actually see our feet," exclaims Noreen.

The first year she ran Noreen wore a wig with tinsel on it.

"But as we've gotten more competitive, we don't dress in anything crazy or flamboyant, just a top and a bottom," says Noreen. "Well, at least most of the time a top."

That's right. In keeping with the clothing-optional spirit of the race, one year Julie and two other Aggies pulled up their tops and flashed the official race photographer.

"We thought it was pretty funny," says Julie. "Then it ended up on some guy from San Diego's Web site."

Even though the Aggies are seeded, and get a choice starting position with the elite runners, the first few miles heading uphill can be clogged with runners and unregistered racers, or bandits, who slip into the race from the sidelines.

"Sometimes it can be dangerous," says Julie. "People just jump off the sidewalk into the race. We're running a six-minute pace, tied together, and somebody who weighs two hundred pounds just jumps in front of us."

Each centipede is allowed two blockers to run ahead clearing the way for the centipede. Dirk and Noreen's husband, Kevin, do that duty. The centipede also is allowed two floaters who can take over if someone has to jump out to tie a shoe or make a pit stop.

While it is fiercely competitive when it comes to beating the Impalas, the female Aggie centipede is unquestionably kinder and more nurturing than the male of the species.

"When the men are running, they're swearing and cussing," Julie says. "In the women's centipede, if we sense someone is hurting we yell, 'Slow down' or put a hand on her back or give her a water sponge. That's what has made our team closer. It's not about us as individuals anymore."

CHAPTER 15

TROTTER

Finding a new way

At twenty-one, Amber Trotter had big plans. On the eve of graduating from college in environmental science, she thought about going to graduate school or maybe teaching at a city high school. Fluent in Spanish, she wanted to explore the world, starting with Cuba. She loved to swim, hike, cycle, and cross-country ski. By any measure, Amber led a full life. There was only one thing missing—running.

As a seventeen-year-old, Amber knew the thrill of standing in the winner's circle. In her senior year of high school, she was a national champion, winning the 2001 Foot Locker Cross-Country Championships with an astounding time of sixteen minutes, twenty-four seconds for 5,000 meters. Her hometown saluted her victory. The school board honored her with a proclamation. And predictions about the Olympics rang true. Amber's victory was all the more notable because of her open struggle with an eating disorder. After high school, she thought she had the problem under control. But anorexia had left its mark. "I've pretty much destroyed my body in a short period of time," Amber explains in a tone absent of regret or resentment.

Amber fell in love with cross-country as a teen. Running through the ocher hills of Northern California's Redwood Valley wine country, she would come back from her morning workout and milk her family's goats. The daughter of two physicians and oldest of three children, Amber played soccer and basketball but not exceptionally well. It wasn't until a friend suggested that she try running that she found her calling. "Racing and training fast is such an exhilarating feeling," she says. "I lose all sense of time and feel both more myself and more a part of everything than at any other time."

Amber could dip into the "zone of pain," as her high school coach used to put it, again and again in her quest to improve. "I went through this phase where I thought, 'I wonder what would happen if I did everything I could to be the best runner I could be?'" Amber recalls. And that's just what she did. She threw herself into hard workouts, including ten-mile runs with every mile faster than the one before, and six-mile runs at a six-minute pace, surging for 300 meters and cruising for 500 meters. She completed workouts twice a day, almost every day.

It paid off. In the tenth grade, Amber finished twentieth at a state cross-country championship. "I proved to myself that I could do something," Amber says. "Prior to running, I had low self-confidence. Running really changed that for me. I was way more confident and self-assured when it came to what I could do."

Amber says she doesn't know how her own eating problem started, but it happened quickly in her sophomore year. "I went from being a healthy-but-thin girl to anorexic in about four months," Amber says. Logging forty to fifty miles a week, she was simply burning more energy than she was taking in. The tall, five-foot-seven teen slipped from 125 pounds to around 100 by the latter half of her sophomore year. "I still don't quite understand how I allowed myself to get sucked in," Amber says. "I feel like it was weak-willed of me. But I honestly wasn't aware that there was anything I should have been resisting."

Focusing on her body as she did only led to dissatisfaction. "You run more and eat less and then, before you know it, your brain chemistry changes and anorexia sets in," Amber says.

As a junior, she made it to the cross-country nationals for the first time. Competing at that elite level, Amber noticed that the best runners were more than just thin. They never seemed to eat. "I don't know if there was anyone who didn't have an eating disorder or wasn't on the brink of an eating disorder," she says. "It was a really stressed-out, really competitive-energy situation. We'd be sitting around at meals without anyone eating anything."

Girls in activities like gymnastics, ballet, and running, where lighter weight often does translate into better performance, are prone to eating disorders. The added risk with teenage girls, too, is their bones are growing, but not yet solid and strong. Anorexia can delay menstruation, resulting in low estrogen levels and weak bones.

Amber should have been taking in three thousand calories a day—almost twice what a sedentary person her age would burn. When she first started losing weight as a sophomore, her times improved, giving her a false boost. Eventually, the weight loss weakened her, physically and emotionally.

After competing in the Foot Locker championships in the winter of her junior year, she felt sapped of energy and was losing interest in running, friends, school. Her teammates noticed, and so did her coach. Drastic steps were taken. Amber was not allowed to compete or train with the team. Bitter and resentful, she knew her life was out of balance. "I thought everyone was being ridiculous," she says, "until I started to realize I had a problem and attempted to address it."

Amber worked with a nutritionist and psychologist, trying to modify her behavior. Not until she got back up to 110 pounds was she permitted to run again. At the start of her senior year, she ran the Great Race of the Great Bay, a 5K event at San Francisco's Golden Gate Park on September 8, 2001. Even with her lost season and struggles, Amber was in top form. She clocked the fastest time that year for any female, girl or woman—seventeen minutes, twenty-one seconds—and burst into tears at the finish. "I felt grateful to be racing again, especially racing well," she says. "In the spring of my junior year, I thought I'd never race again, so to come back like that was a tremendous blessing."

Her senior year turned into one long winning streak—state champion, regional champion, national champion. At the Foot Locker championships on December 8, 2001, at Walt Disney World in Orlando, Amber set a course record, beating the next runner by forty seconds. "Being as fast as I was that season was a total shocker for me," Amber recalls. "All season I kept waiting to burn out and watch everyone else run past me."

Heading into spring track, Amber suffered recurring pain in her backside. She tried to ignore it, but couldn't. She laid off training for two weeks, but the problem persisted. Doctors deduced that her piriformis muscle, deep in her buttocks, was irritating her sciatic nerve. It was serious enough to sideline her again.

When it came time to head off to college, Amber stunned the running world by bypassing a big-name school like the University of Oregon for Middlebury College in Vermont, which competed in the NCAA Division III. Amber picked Middlebury for its academic excellence. She also liked the running coach, who had produced a championship team, and was impressed with the college's athletic facilities. And there was something thankfully missing at Middlebury—all the media scrutiny, pressure, and internal competition that came with elite collegiate sports.

Privately, too, her choice was part of a larger plan. "I thought I wanted to pursue running after college, maybe go to the Olympics," Amber says. "I thought it was in my best interest to take it easy in college, not get burnt out." She knew all too well the pressure on young athletes, the miles of training, the racing, the travel, the speed work. And since distance runners usually don't peak until closer to thirty, why not throttle back through college? "I wanted to focus more on academics and developing as a human being," Amber says. "I thought after college, I'd really get down to serious running."

That was the plan—if only her body had played along. She suffered chronic pain from her sciatic nerve, part of her complicated injury. Amber was forced to sit out her first year of athletics at Middlebury. Her second year, she tried again to run cross-country. In her second race, she felt a new kind of pain that left her screaming. "I didn't know what was wrong with me," Amber says. "It felt like I had pulled a muscle deep inside." X-rays showed that she had hairline fractures in her pelvis and sacrum. Further testing showed that Amber's bones were not as dense as they should be for a young woman. Years of anorexia had left her with osteoporosis. "I have the bones of a seventy-year-old woman," she says. Worse yet, "My bones will shatter if I start running at a competitive level."

Her college running career was over before it started. "It is impossible to determine whether or not my body could once again handle intense training," she says. She would like to try again in a few years, but for now all she can handle are a few miles of light jogging, a far cry from the intense, constant poundings of her youth.

Nowadays, Amber swims a few miles almost every day. For the high school girl who used to be the fastest in the country, it's been an adjustment. Yet, even if Amber could get back the life she had, she's not sure she wants it. "If I got a scholarship to study abroad, would I turn it down to train? Probably not."

Running can be a selfish companion, as Amber knows too well. To accomplish all that she did, she had to spend less time with friends, family, and herself.

"So was it worth it? For me, yes, because I gained so much from the experience," Amber says.

"If I had things to do over again, I wouldn't change a thing. But for many people, what I sacrificed wouldn't have been worth what I lost."

CHAPTER 16

WESSEL

Dressing women runners

Women are square, men are rectangular.

Ellen Wessel had not yet figured that out when she bought her first pair of running shorts at a Herman's Sporting Goods warehouse sale in 1974. All she wanted was a pair of shorts that fit across her hips but didn't seize up in the crotch. So she bought a cotton canvas pair that was way too big everywhere else. "There was this huge wad of excess fabric bunching up between my legs," Ellen says.

The problem was twofold: First, women have wider hips than men, and the distance from waist to crotch is longer for a woman than for a man.

The second part of the problem: In the mid-1970s, apparel makers just didn't care. Either that, or they didn't see the potential in sports apparel designed for women—a potentially huge market as millions of girls began participating in sports under the recently passed Title IX.

Ellen Wessel wasn't sure about the size of the market, but she was sure she could sell some shorts to women like herself who had become obsessed with running.

What started in an apartment with a $75 Singer sewing

machine and modified McCall's patterns became a million-dollar business. Her company, Moving Comfort, would fight off bankruptcy, face the headaches of overseas production, and fold into a multinational apparel giant. Yet still Ellen runs the show.

Ellen had glimpsed the future, way back in 1974—women did want shorts that fit. But she didn't see how many colors they'd want them in, or how concerned they'd be that shorts and tops matched, or how important a comfortable bra would be to them—or that women's active apparel would become a $5 billion-a-year industry.

"People really thought it was a gimmick—that women could possibly need something different than a man," she recalls at Moving Comfort's chic, modern showroom, which seems as if it could be on Seventh Avenue, but is actually in a suburban industrial park in northern Virginia.

Stretchy sample shorts, tops, bras, and pants, made from the latest synthetics, hang in color-coordinated rows: lavender, cornflower blue, and citrus green. There are tiny flowers too, patterns named Freesia, a larger, modish floral called Starburst and Tango, a green-and-white background dotted by red and purple shapes that resemble a backward version of Nike's signature swoosh.

There is the Maia Bra, a tribute to the Greek goddess, and the Grace Bra named, in part, for one of Ellen's horses. Bras are also dedicated to the daughters of Moving Comfort staff: Larkin, Lucia, and Caitlin among them.

It's a long way from the seventies, when Ellen was a purist. All that mattered was that a pair of shorts did its job. But as the market for women's running apparel grew, women were demanding color and style, too.

"The first shorts were in soft cottons and nylon in colors like powder blue and yellow. In the beginning it was completely about fit," she says. "Having the shorts match the shoes was the first thing we began to get requests for."

At first she thought it was silly, but over time she began to understand why fashion is important.

"Enjoying how your workout clothes look and feel is highly motivating. How you look affects how you feel, your motivation and your energy level. It's all part of the same thing. The first thing is it has to fit, but it also has to look good. The aesthetics have become extremely important."

When Ellen began running, she stood out. It was 1974 and she was trying to kick a smoking habit and improve a lifestyle that landed her in the doctor's office too often. She tried jogging around a tiny indoor track at the YMCA, but it hurt her ankles.

Another woman from the Y invited her to run outside. "That was a novel idea," says Ellen. "Being a woman running outside, in shorts, was not normal in 1974. Being honked at and harassed was."

Running soon dominated her life. She began to enter local races and by 1976 was running up to seventy miles a week. She ran the Marine Corps Marathon that year. At one point her doctor put her in a cast when she would not lay off long enough to let an injury heal. "I have a strong recollection of depression when I had an injury and couldn't run."

She'd always been passionate in everything she'd done. Raised in White Plains, New York, she was a college freshman in 1970 when the National Guard gunned down antiwar protesters at Kent State University in Ohio. She campaigned for George McGovern in 1972. ("We were angry, passionate students," she says.) By 1973, she had moved to Washington, D.C., "to change the world."

In 1974, she was working in the Washington bureau of the *Philadelphia Bulletin* (official title: "Girl Friday"), loving the job but smoking too much. She had already quit once and gained weight: "I decided I'd rather be skinny even if it meant dying early."

When she wound up at her doctor's office for the second time in months, Ellen changed her mind. "It was a pivotal moment," she says. "I decided that the only way to keep off cigarettes permanently was to declare myself an athlete and start running."

Once she became a runner, she was obsessed. Before each race, she warmed up in training shoes then switched to lighter flats for the race. "Every ounce mattered. That was my whole life," she says. "Running and sleeping."

On training runs, she and her running partner at the time, Valerie Nye, would fantasize about quitting their jobs to start their own running-apparel company. That way, they figured, they could devote even more time to running.

In 1977, Ellen did just that. She left her job at the Department of Housing and Urban Development after discovering she possessed an attribute that doesn't work for a government bureaucrat, but is crucial for an entrepreneur. "I didn't like working for other people," she explains.

So she entered the garment business, not knowing much about garments or business. Valerie, who was doing public relations work, had grown up sewing, but neither had any experience designing clothes or working with patterns.

Their new company, Moving Comfort, set up shop in Valerie's apartment, with the sewing machine and the McCall's patterns, and began making shorts out of fabric they bought at a sewing shop. The company sold its creations to a new crop of specialty running stores with names like the Human Race, Track Shack, and Foot Works. The stores were owned by runners and, like Ellen, they were trying to make running a way of life, and a livelihood.

The business struggled and Valerie, who was married with a

young child, bowed out. Ellen, living on savings and a small inheritance, moved the company to her apartment.

Soon after, Ellen's younger brother, Lewis, went on a double date with a man who used to be Ellen's boyfriend. Ellen's ex was now seeing another runner, Elizabeth Goeke. He had given Elizabeth a pair of Moving Comfort shorts, but she returned them because they didn't fit.

Elizabeth was working as an apprentice tailor at a Washington department store and told Ellen's brother she'd be happy to give Moving Comfort some feedback. Ellen called her immediately and the two began working on new patterns. They ran together in test shorts and signed on with a contract manufacturer in South Carolina. Six months later, Elizabeth quit her job and became an equal partner in Moving Comfort.

"I was just lucky I found Elizabeth so quickly. I don't know how I would have done it alone," says Ellen. "I'm a collaborator. I like sharing the joy and the struggle. When I see friends who are sole proprietors I think how un-fun that would be not to have a business partner."

After four years in business, Moving Comfort's sales hit $1 million. Larger players noticed the new market too, and were flooding stores with active apparel for women. Nearly forced into bankruptcy, Moving Comfort's staff dropped from twenty-one to ten. Ellen and Elizabeth renegotiated bank loans, and fired the office cleaning company. They cleaned the toilets.

It took several years, but eventually much of the excess competition was squeezed out. Moving Comfort was among those left standing. "The truth is we didn't know how to quit," says Ellen.

As the company grew it branched out from shorts to tops and jackets, including a memorable bright orange terry-cloth warm-up suit from the late 1970s that remains on display in the corporate offices today.

Moving Comfort steered clear of bras for years because it shared a team of sales representatives with JogBra, the pioneering sports bra maker. After Playtex acquired JogBra in 1990, Moving Comfort entered that business too.

Now bras are its largest-selling category. Sports bras have grown high tech. New fabrics and structural design are constantly being used to enhance the two main properties of a good bra: compression, which flattens breasts, and encapsulation, which contains them. Moving Comfort has trademarked a system called DriLayer that defines Moving Comfort garments designed to wick moisture away from the body.

The company's best-selling bras are in size D and DD, says Ellen. "For these women this is their most important piece of equipment."

Ellen acknowledges she has little need for a bra at all, and is not of much help in product testing for compression and encapsulation. But she does have sensitive skin and considers herself the resident expert on chafe.

Beyond the challenge of designing stylish and technically sound bras, Moving Comfort has been swept up in the forces of globalization. By the mid-1990s, more and more U.S. garment manufacturers closed their doors because of new competition from other countries. Moving Comfort was having trouble finding domestic manufacturers. Large U.S. competitors were adapting more easily to offshore production. And the company was too small to monitor labor conditions in overseas factories, particularly in China, says Ellen.

"It's ironic, but as a small company with every intention of enhancing the quality of people's lives, we could not afford to oversee working conditions," she says.

So in August 2002, Ellen and Elizabeth took on another partner, Russell Corp., the huge athletic apparel manufacturer. Ellen and Elizabeth continue to manage the Moving Comfort brand within Russell.

As Moving Comfort has grown and matured, so have its founders. They are both divorced, have boyfriends, and are "happily single."

"Elizabeth and I have been moving along with the baby boomers," says Ellen. "I'm fitter than I was in my twenties, but gravity changes things whether we like it or not."

Ellen still runs, but she also does weight training and yoga, rides horses, and kayaks, something at least six days a week.

"Everything is in moderation now, and that's the way it has to be if you want to do this for the rest of your life," she says. "I was living on the edge in the 1970s. For my friends and me it was about how much you could push yourself before you got injured. You're looking for excitement in your twenties and thirties, and looking for peace in your forties and fifties."

Still, there is a difference between running and a yoga class.

"When you're running you don't have to think about what you're doing. And that's when you can really think about whatever problems you're up against," says Ellen. "I wouldn't be in business if it weren't for running. It has given me a such a different self-awareness about possibility and overcoming obstacles."

CHAPTER 17

Midori
SPERANDEO

Pregnancy, babies, and running

Midori Sperandeo peered at the black-and-white ultrasound image and tried to make out the outline of her baby. There it was: the child she and her husband Leonard thought they could never have. Five years before, a fertility expert had told Midori she had "low-quality eggs," making pregnancy remote. But she had beaten the odds. Midori was more than eighteen weeks pregnant and the pulsing gray spot on the screen was a heartbeat.

For Midori, having a baby was just another unexpected turn in a life full of twists. A few years back, as she was nearing thirty, she started running to get in shape. Working as a television reporter in Sacramento, she jogged a mile a day, then two, then three. She joined a local running club, got up to fifty miles a week and, four months after starting serious training, entered her first marathon—and won.

News of her feat spread through Sacramento's running community. On an assignment covering a local triathlon, Midori was stopped at a prerace pasta dinner by a tall, lean runner. "Aren't you the woman who won her first marathon?" he asked. There was,

Midori recalls, "instant chemistry." A year later, she married the runner, who became her coach as well.

Midori dreamed of making the Olympic Trials, and Leonard, a serious runner since high school and a former college coach, hoped to guide her there. Midori had a ferocious work ethic as an athlete. Leonard thought his job as her coach was to slow her down. "There are a few athletes if they don't have a coach, they'll kill themselves," Leonard said. "She falls into that *go-go-go, run-run-run, more-more-more* category."

It might seem foolhardy for a novice to set her sights on the Olympic Trials. But in 1999, three years into running, Midori finished the Chicago Marathon in two hours, forty-nine minutes, and forty-six seconds—she had qualified for the 2000 Olympic Trials.

Midori, who has a short, light frame and muscular legs, never seriously expected to make the U.S. team her first time around. Indeed, she finished in the middle of the pack. But the excitement of running with the best women in the country was a thrill all its own. Coming off that high, Midori had another surprise—she was pregnant.

Now, lying on her back in the doctor's office, she was mesmerized by the ultrasound image. How many baby scrapbooks start with that first ultrasound photo, scarcely decipherable, but proof of a child's arrival?

"Does the baby have running legs?" Leonard anxiously asked the ultrasound technician. "Is it a boy or girl?"

"Uh . . . a girl," the technician said, hesitating. "Excuse me, I have to leave for a minute."

Moments later, Midori's doctor entered the room. Her manner was grave. The ultrasound showed "multiple abnormalities," she said. Unfamiliar medical words and unnatural descriptions floated past the dazed couple. *Omphalocele. A sac outside the body holding the liver. A severely curved spine. Problems with the placenta, brain, and heart.*

The doctor said to Midori and Leonard that at some point, the fetus would die. From miracle to tragedy, just like that.

At home, Midori tried to process what had just happened. She sent out an SOS on a Web site for mothers of children with omphalocele. She now knew her fetus was malformed, with organs protruding from the abdominal wall near the base of the placenta. But there were other complications, summed up with vague totality by the doctor as *body stock anomaly*. "I just don't know what the right thing is to do," Midori asked in an online plea. "I don't even know if there is anything I can do."

Her doctor told the couple there was a zero chance of survival. None. Midori and Leonard made the difficult decision to end the pregnancy. "I will always have such a sad place in my heart about that decision and the baby," Midori explains. "What's sad is I never got to see her. I never got to see her face. I don't know what she looks like."

They had named their daughter Mikili and they grieved for her as any parents would mourn the loss of a child. Running became Midori's escape, a salve for her soul. Her daily workouts gave her day structure, something to do between waking up and falling into fitful sleep. *Eyes open, shoes on, run.* No time to languish in bed in the dark.

Outdoors, Midori was alone with her thoughts. Her legs turned like the quick clicks of a metronome. Her breathing was slow, steady, and soothing. And her mind was always on the baby whose face she couldn't see. "I wanted her soul to forgive me," Midori says. Midori always felt passionate about her running. But now it took on a whole new meaning. Running over so many miles was a journey deeper and deeper into herself. And the more she ran, the stronger she became in body and mind.

In time, Midori allowed herself to think of the future, to dream again. She wanted to run another marathon. She wanted another chance at the Olympic Trials. "I wanted to make something good happen in my life after something so bad," she says.

Many women runners come back from pregnancy stronger than before. Some think it has to do with the forced rest that comes in the last months of pregnancy. Others think it's tied to changes in hormone levels. Whatever the reason, Midori was running faster than ever. "I could run paces I never dreamed I could do before," Midori says. On long, twenty-mile training runs, she maintained a pace of six minutes, nine seconds a mile. In a 10K, she hit a new personal best, finishing in thirty-five minutes, nineteen seconds.

In early 2002, a little more than a half year after losing her baby, Midori ran the Las Vegas International Marathon on a still, clear February day when everything seemed to go right. She won with a time of two hours, forty-one minutes, and fifty-one seconds, a personal best and once again fast enough to qualify for the Olympic Trials. After the race, Midori told a local newspaper reporter, "I thought of the baby, that I would do this for her. This makes everything come full circle."

The Olympic Trials weren't all she dreamed of. She and Leonard still wanted a child, but the thought of trying again scared Midori. *Would she be able to conceive? Would she lose this baby too?* Leonard, who'd spent a lonely childhood in foster care, ached for children. Midori, however, now had the Olympic Trials in two years to worry about. "There is a fear," Midori says. "Are you going to be able to come back? Are you going to be able to get your body back? But something inside of you just tells you to do it."

She had scheduled an appointment with a fertility specialist a few months later when she learned she was pregnant.

Midori ran through her entire pregnancy. In her first trimester, she trained an hour a day, all the while monitoring her heart rate so she didn't overdo it.

As her pregnancy progressed, she cut back her workouts to forty-five minutes, then thirty minutes. Her pace slowed too, dropping to eight-minute miles, then ten-minute miles, then something akin to a brisk waddle. And when it felt too uncomfortable to run on land, Midori went to a pool and ran in place in the water. Midori was jogging with a friend when she felt her first contractions. Thirty-seven hours later—without anything to blunt the pain—she gave birth to a son, Koby. Of her marathon labor, Midori says, "It was the most suffering I've ever done!"

Midori had only eight months to train for the Olympic Trials. This time around it was harder to rebound from pregnancy and the physical strain of having carried a baby to term. Part of the problem, she believes, was her decision to breast-feed her son while running up to a hundred miles a week. "I was very tired," Midori says. "I crashed and burned a lot on runs."

But her times were good. On twenty-mile training runs, a critical gauge of progress for marathon runners, she could still run at a mile pace of six minutes, four seconds. "That was great for me," Midori recalled. "But for the next week or two, I'd practically die on a four-miler."

What was going on? Other than commonsense conclusions that mixing a newborn with rigorous training will wear you down, Midori could find very little information. She could find no books, no Web sites, no studies on "marathon training and the lactating runner." She was in uncharted territory. "For the most part, I was falling apart," Midori says. Never did it occur to her to stop nursing. "Koby was more important to me than my marathon."

Arriving in St. Louis for the 2004 Olympic Marathon Trials, Midori was nagged by the thought that even if she was mentally prepared, physically she wasn't ready. "Too many things were going wrong," she said. Doctors had told her that her hormones could be out of whack. Her heartbeat, too, had been irregular.

With her husband, baby son, and mother to cheer her, Midori got off to a rough start and never bounced back. Her splits were way off. By mile ten, "my legs felt like noodles," she recalls. By mile thirteen, she spied Leonard off on the side of the road and ran toward him. "I don't know what to do," she implored. Leonard reached for her arm, knowing that any physical contact with a competitor would disqualify her. "You're pretty much done," he gently said. She had gone out too hard and paid the price. Leonard did not want her to hurt herself by plodding for another thirteen miles. It was a bad day, falling in one of the troughs of her training cycles. "I was extremely relieved that it was over," Midori says. "The pressure was off and I could do what I wanted."

With two Olympic Marathon Trials under her belt, Midori saw no reason why she shouldn't try for a third shot in 2008. But in what would now become a familiar pattern, she would have to scale back her training for a half year. In the spring of 2005, Midori was pregnant again.

Leonard had faith, too, that his wife could rebound for another Olympic bid, even though she would be forty-two the next time around. Many elite runners think of retirement at that age. Midori, on the other hand, didn't start serious running until she was thirty. As far as she was concerned, she was only getting started. "If you've been running since high school, you max out by the time you're thirty-eight. You're done," Midori says. "I'm glad I started later. I don't have all the emotional baggage of a lot of runners who ran in college."

But the mother-runner act can get tricky sometimes. Keeping up with a toddler is exhausting work for the sleep-deprived. And it seems that Koby is a walking Petri dish for germs that cause sniffles and coughs. Without fail, every time Koby gets sick, so does Midori.

It's harder, too, to focus on training. To get her mileage in, Midori will run eight miles in the morning, logging another four in the evening. It has helped to have a husband who was also her coach. Instead of hearing the harried-husband lament of, "Why are you going out running?"—Midori will get, "Why aren't you going out running?"

Olympics or not, Midori has a lifetime of motherhood ahead of her. Like any parent, she hopes her kids will share the passion she and Leonard have for running. And maybe the day will come when Koby will want to know, "What's a marathon, Mommy?"

Midori will pull out his baby scrapbook and show him pictures from the Olympic Trials in St. Louis when he was eight months old and watching with his grandmother from the sidelines. Then she will tell her son what it feels like to go after something so great, challenging, and large—the commitment to a dream, the hours of work, the reward of the race. "All these things bring such a spark to your life," she says, "and I don't want him to miss out on that."

CHAPTER 18

Students Run
PHILLY STYLE

Running to a brighter future

The streets are tough in this part of West Philadelphia. Boarded-up homes, sealed shops with metal grates, and vacant lots line both sides of once-grand Lancaster Avenue. Men cluster at corners, wordlessly approaching cars that slow to a stop.

And yet, twice a week, two Catholic schoolgirls in Peter Pan collars and plaid skirts change into silky shorts and running shoes, emerge from Our Mother of Sorrows school, and run through this troubled neighborhood on their way to the city's riverside oasis, Fairmount Park.

Ashley Ethengain and Fitimah White trot past the towering spires of the heavy, stone church and the nineteenth-century cemetery that surrounds it. They hit their stride as they head toward the Moe Better Barber Shop, the Dollar-n-More, and Sir Richard's Tavern. Near the Sunshine market, where men forage for food in a Dumpster, they turn toward the park, on their way to another future.

Five months ago, the two seventh-graders couldn't run a quarter mile around the cemetery. Now, they are up to fourteen miles. They are training to run the Philadelphia Marathon in a few months. "The first day I ran past two trees on the block, then I stopped," says Fitimah.

"Now I feel stronger," says Ashley. "I can push myself harder, for as long as it takes now."

At twelve, Fitimah towers over thirteen-year-old Ashley. That kind of thing happens at this age. But they have been best friends for years. They both wear their hair back in braids and they both take dance lessons—Ashley favors ballet, Fitimah is more into hip-hop. Both live at home with their mothers and four brothers and sisters.

They are on the cusp. One minute, the girls are giggling and dancing to "Cotton-Eyed Joe" on a boom box. The next minute, they are confident and worldly, striving to be taken as the adults they will soon be. The new school year has just begun, but they are anxious about next year when scholarships will be awarded that would allow them to continue in private school at West Catholic High School.

Running, they hope, just might help.

This spring they joined Students Run Philly Style, a nonprofit program intended to build discipline and confidence in inner-city kids by taking on an outrageous goal—running a marathon. Across the city, nine teams—with a total of seventy kids—were formed, each with a set of adult mentors coaching the teens toward their goal, one step at a time.

When Ashley and Fitimah take to the streets, Paula Hawkins, a reading instructor at Our Mother of Sorrows, is right there with them. "They both come from rough neighborhoods that are really drug-infested. There's a lot of gun activity. This gives them something to do and keeps them out of trouble," says Paula.

A basketball player in high school, Paula put on thirty pounds her first year at college and became a runner to get those pounds off. "I'm a seasonal runner. I run in the spring and summer to get in shape when the winter clothes come off," she says. "Then I go into hibernation again in the winter."

While she may be a fair-weather runner, she is a dedicated teacher who quit a career in retail management to teach at the inner-city Catholic school. "I figured if I had to work, I might as well do something I enjoy, and I enjoy being around children. You get so much out of seeing them blossom, and to know maybe I played a little part."

It can be a struggle. When Ashley and Fitimah started running with Paula in the spring there were twelve other students in the group. By the end of the summer, only Ashley and Fitimah and a boy were running regularly.

"When it got hot and everybody dropped out, it was just me and Fitimah getting dark and hot," says Ashley.

Many days it was just Paula and the girls. They developed a routine: Run to Fairmount Park on Tuesday and Thursdays and around the cemetery on Saturday. Sometimes they went out to dinner or lunch. "We have gotten so much closer because we have struggled through all those miles together," says Paula.

Ashley and Fitimah feel the same. "We can tell her everything," says Fitimah. "She's like a mom to us."

For Paula, who has two sons, the runs bring her into a different world. "They talk about boys and say, 'Don't you think he's cute, Miss Hawkins?' and I say, 'Guess what? You know I don't want to hear that kind of talk.' But they're at that age."

For inspiration, the Philadelphia runners need only look to Los Angeles, where the idea of heading off teenage trouble with a marathon was hatched. Students Run Philly Style is modeled on Students Run L.A., which has trained thousands of kids to run the Los Angeles Marathon with volunteer teacher-coaches. Up to two thousand students a year train with 250 coaches, and 97 percent finish the race, the same rate of completion for the entire field of twenty thousand runners. More important, 90 percent of the seniors who complete the marathon graduate from high school. The graduation rate for the L.A. Unified School District is 65 percent.

The idea behind Students Run L.A. came from Harry Shabazian, a teacher in the city continuation high school system for problem students, who ran the marathon for the first time in 1986. "I found the experience tremendously difficult but very rewarding," Harry says. "I felt that the kids I was working with particularly in East L.A. could benefit from this. So when I came back to class the following day, I was hobbling around and one of the guys said, 'Are you going to do this next year?' And I said, 'Yeah. You interested?' Lo and behold I got seven to give it a try."

Of that first seven, who lied about their age claiming to be eighteen, six completed the marathon. The one who didn't was a girl who had stayed out until 3 A.M. the morning of the race, and who surrendered at mile ten.

Harry felt he was on to something. "I was working with kids who already had little self-esteem," he says. "I got them to give it a try and you could see them begin to develop a sense of hope. That is what the marathon experience does."

Two other teachers in the system heard about what Harry was doing and started their own training groups. The idea grew, and in 1993, Students Run L.A. became a full-scale nonprofit organization backed by the Los Angeles Unified School District.

After several years, leaders of Students Run L.A. began to notice that while girls and boys were signing up in equal numbers, the girls dropped out almost twice as fast as the boys. "The girls were struggling," says Marsha Charney, executive director of

Students Run L.A. "It seems the girls have a tougher time when the miles get longer than boys do. Also, culturally, girls are more apt to be kept home by their mothers. At the last minute they can't make it to a race because they need to help with the younger children."

To combat the dropout rate, Students Run L.A. created Girls Day, a girls-only run where pediatricians and nutritionists are invited to answer the girls' questions about health and running. Coaches were taught to pay closer attention, and the dropout rate for girls and boys is now more balanced.

During the year, Students Run L.A. sponsors groups in local races around the city, many of them 5Ks and 10Ks, where kids get to meet other young runners and develop a sense of camaraderie. But the marathon remains the centerpiece of Students Run L.A. Anything less would not have the same impact, Harry believes. "You can get your buddies together and go out and do a 10K and that's nice, but the minute you tell people you did a marathon they see you in a different light."

Harry once ran the marathon with a three-hundred-pound boy who took nine and a half hours to finish. "All of us emphasize to our runners that if you take that first step, do everything in your power to also take that last step."

Programs modeled after Students Run L.A. are now up and running in Oakland, Portland, and in Philadelphia, where Paula shares Harry's belief that taking one step can lead to so much more. "We try to show that if you can put your mind to something it carries over to other things in their lives," Paula says. "Maybe they will think, 'If I can run five miles maybe I can get a C in this science class if I just try.'"

Paula already sees changes. At first, she says, Fitimah was tough. "She was aloof. She had a slight attitude. It was difficult to tell her anything. Now she's gotten so much better. You're able to tell her things and she takes it constructively. She doesn't give you attitude."

Ashley used to be quiet. "She's come out of her shell. Now she talks a lot. She's much more outgoing."

While Our Mother of Sorrows is something of a fortress in a rough part of town, it is still middle school, which can be scary in even the best neighborhoods. But Ashley and Fitimah are learning to run through the pressure of teen cool like another side stitch.

"People say we're crazy," says Fitimah.

"Half of the class is cheering for us and the other half is jealous saying, 'I'd never run track," says Ashley.

She lifts her chin and sets her shoulders. "I say to them, 'Well that's you, and I'm not you.'"

CHAPTER 19

CANNON

Four-legged running partners

Picture this: three runners on a dirt road in the Colorado high country. From behind you see their legs high-stepping and ponytails swishing in rhythm. The ponytail in the middle is long and blonde and belongs to forty-four-year-old Colleen Cannon. The two on either end are long and gray and belong to Arabian horses named Demi and Rafiki.

Some people run with their dogs, and others with kids in strollers. Colleen runs with her horses. Along Magnolia Road, neighbors have gotten used to the sight of them on their daily jog. But long-distance runners from around the world who train in the remote backwoods above Boulder, a lung-expanding eight thousand feet above sea level, do a double-take whenever Colleen and her horses pass by. Sometimes, Colleen will tease her audience. She'll grab onto leather straps on each horse's bareback pad and lift herself up as the horses break into a canter. Her soles barely brush the ground as she takes off with what seems like superhero speed. A team of Japanese runners were so incredulous they filmed her to show everyone back home. Through a translator, they told her, "You're the fastest woman we've ever seen!"

To listen to Colleen, there are no finer running partners than Demi and Rafiki. What's most surprising the first time you see them is how natural they look together—why, it occurs to you, doesn't everyone run with horses? Colleen runs shoulder to shoulder with the horses in tight formation. Their pace is steady, with the horses reacting to Colleen's commands and movements as if she was the lead mare of a herd. Never once has a horse stomped a hoof on Colleen's foot or tripped her.

"It's just plain fun," Colleen enthuses. "They set a good pace, they're never tired . . . and they have their own sense of talking. I don't ask, 'How was your day?' But you can tell how they're feeling."

Colleen, a retired professional triathlete, is a veritable life force who's made it her business to share some of that with other women. She organizes adventure weeks under the name "Women's Quest." One week she and her staff might take women into the Rockies to teach them how to snowshoe and cross-country ski; another time they might cycle through Napa Valley or meditate on the beach in Hawaii. She embraces life and then makes you want to give it a hug too. She uses words like "joy bubbles" and "happy molecules" but then stops herself, saying, "That sounds too 'Boulder-ish,' doesn't it?"

She got into running with horses because riding Demi was too hard. "I'd get on her and she wouldn't stop," Colleen recalls. "I was like, 'Where are the brakes?'" Colleen had grown up riding horses, but when she bought Demi in 1992, it was her first attempt at training a horse.

Demi came at a turning point for Colleen. She was switching from one job to another—from professional triathlete to organizer of fitness retreats.

Colleen stumbled into triathlons. A college boyfriend had signed up for a triathlon in Oxford, Maryland. The year was 1980.

Colleen was an athlete at Auburn University, where she was on the swimming, cross-country, and track teams. She tagged along from Alabama just for the fun of it. The night before the triathlon, she helped the race director stuff packets for competitors. To repay her, he told her she could enter the triathlon for free. But how, Colleen wanted to know. "I didn't raise any money," she tried to explain to him. "Don't you have to sign up sponsors to pay you pennies per mile to raise money for charity?"

After someone explained the difference between "triathlon" and "walkathon," Colleen still had trouble with the concept. This became clear after the first event—a 2.4-mile open-water swim. "I was first out of the water," she explains. "I was clapping for everyone, yelling, 'Yeah! Good for you!'"

Er, Colleen. This is a race.

The twenty-mile run was a struggle. Colleen was a middle-distance runner at Auburn. Luckily she found "three cute guys" to provide a pleasant distraction. "We just talked the whole way," she says.

The final fifty-mile bike leg was downright comical. Colleen had brought her bike to Maryland, thinking she'd follow her boyfriend as a spectator. It had upright handlebars, a big basket, horn, and streamers. On race day, Colleen had a stash of race food in her basket: a six-pack of Coke, a peanut-butter-and-jelly sandwich, and a package of Little Debbie oatmeal cookies. "I didn't know if it was going to take me one day or two," Colleen recalls. "At every aid station, I'd put my kickstand down and eat some bananas and cookies."

Stuffed and exhausted, with not to mention a very sore crotch, she saw a tent with cots and immediately crashed onto one. Workers surged to her. "Are you okay? What's wrong," people said, swarming.

"I'm just going to rest here," she said, taking a small pillow out of her bike basket. The volunteers shooed her away, explaining that this was the medical tent, not a napping station.

Despite her missteps, Colleen finished second. "I vowed I would never do another one," she says. "Never again. I thought these people were nuts."

She returned to Auburn, where she was working on her master's degree in exercise physiology. "People started calling me, saying, 'Let's do another one,'" she says.

Colleen caved in and discovered something else about triathlons: prize money. Companies, anxious to promote interest in triathlons, were willing to sponsor competitors. Colleen was picked up by Nike, which underwrote her travel expenses. The bike manufacturer Specialized sent her a bike. She also got endorsements from Pioneer Electronics and Hind clothing.

She competed in shorter triathlons that had a one-mile swim, twenty-five-mile cycle, and 10K run. Taken separately, her skills in swimming, cycling, and running were not world class. But taken together, she became stellar. "I wasn't a good-enough swimmer, biker, or runner," she says, "but I became a really good triathlete."

For a decade after college, Colleen earned a living as a professional athlete. She competed in about twenty events a year, earning $45,000 her first year out and winning the world championship in 1984. She traveled around the country and world, competing in China, New Zealand, Europe, Brazil, Japan, and Canada. She caught the wave of triathlon popularity and rode it all the way to the beach.

But by 1992, the competitive life was wearing her down. She wanted to try something new. "You have to do what gives you joy," she explains. "And this wasn't fun anymore."

She was thirty-two. She wanted to give back something. Her idea: retreats for women. "I wanted to use sports more as a vehicle to learn how to feel good about yourself," Colleen says. That way, "You wake up a whole place in your life."

Each weeklong Women's Quest retreat included training in sports like running, biking, or orienteering, with extra servings of "soul food" like yoga, meditation, or hot-spring soaking. She planned a special week for introducing women to horseback riding around the mountains near Steamboat Springs.

Colleen had grown up with well-trained quarter horses. But Demi—short for Demeter, the Greek earth goddess—was out of control. "Unrideable," Colleen declares. "She was crazy wild. She wouldn't go right or left. I thought I'm safer on the ground. I didn't know how to train a horse."

She spent months running alongside Demi, working on voice commands as well as leading her from the ground. Today, Demi is as docile as a trained dog. With Rafiki, a slightly pudgy mixed Arabian, Colleen takes her horses all over the state, looking for less-traveled trails. They've gone on five-hour runs in Rocky Mountain National Park, across the Continental Divide, and around Winter Park. Their daily runs may stretch for ten miles. Sometimes on long uphill climbs, Colleen will take a breather and jump on Demi's back.

Late one summer day, in a secluded pasture of tall, sweet grass below pine-wrapped Winegar Ridge, Colleen led Demi and Rafiki in single-file. She leaned her tanned shoulder into Demi's gray freckled one. The horse responded by shadowing her movement. Colleen can think of no better way to run. "When you're in your zone, you start to click and you're flying," she explains. "Horses lift your heart."

CHAPTER 20

NG

Born with a runner's soul

The doors to the school swing open at 3:05 P.M. Seven-year-old Taylor Ng steps up to her mother, Nancy, and hands over her backpack.

"Taylor, do you need to run?" Nancy asks.

It is not a question of whether Taylor wants to run. With Taylor, there is a need to run.

A smile pushes through Taylor's retainer wire and she turns to face the blacktop. Nancy, as she does most days after school, looks down at the secondhand on her watch.

"Go."

Taylor blasts off from the chain-link fence, pounds across a stretch of asphalt, circles past the jungle gym, and heads back to Nancy.

Thirty seconds.

At school there are kids who are good in art or music, kids who make jokes, and kids who write poems. Taylor runs. Around school she is known as Taylor-the-girl-who-runs.

Already she has powerful calves, and her shoulders move in an athletic rhythm with her legs, even when she walks. There are a lot of kids who like to run, but Taylor is not a hyper, sloppy kid runner. She is controlled like a cheetah, and stays close to the ground.

"I like to be fast," says Taylor. "When I run fast, it seems like the wind is blowing right on my face."

Nancy can always tell when she's about to bolt. "She gets this little flash in her eye. Every time."

Taylor plays soccer, tennis, and Little League baseball, but her top game is tag.

"One. Two. Three. Get off of my father's apple tree," Taylor commands her tag mates, who are clinging to the security of the playground bench that is base.

"Back. Back," they plead as Taylor steps away slowly, crouching, ready to spring should one dare make a break. Gabrielle finally sprints off to the right, but she gets less than two yards away, before Taylor swoops down. Michael darts past and is tagged flat in the back. Sylvia tries to go head-on, but Taylor catches her on the wrist.

The second-grade tag crowd was once larger, but now it is down to a handful of specialists. "Sometimes I don't like it when there are too many people," says Taylor. "Sometimes they just wander around."

Even those who are still in the game are easy prey, but Taylor works with what she has.

"When we play tag, usually I have to get them," she says. "Or they have to get me with five people. I say, 'Hey that's not fair.' They say it's fair because I'm faster."

Taylor got off to a fast start. She began to walk at seven months, if only to keep up with her sister Spencer. When their girls were still toddlers, Nancy and her husband, Arthur, lived in an apartment complex on Chicago's South Side. They worked long hours and when they returned at night, the family took walks down the halls of their building's corridors. The girls laughed and giggled as they ran and tumbled down the halls.

"If in any way we encouraged running, it was only that we smiled to see them having so much fun," says Arthur.

By the time she was three, Taylor's Montessori teacher reported that she was regularly outrunning kids three years older. She gave Nancy and Arthur the name of a track club.

When Spencer went to elementary school, Taylor came with her mother each morning to drop her sister off. After the big kids were in school, Taylor demanded that Nancy race her back across the playground to the car. Nancy used to like to wear clogs, but she had to switch to sneakers.

When Taylor was in first grade, the fifth-grade safeties noticed her daily after-school dash. At the end of the year, one of the fifth grade's best and fastest, Ryan Black, challenged Taylor to a race across the playground. He beat her by a hair. The next day there was a rematch. They tied.

"She is so small and her legs are so low to the ground it gives you the illusion that she's even faster than she is," Ryan explains.

Taylor constantly challenges Nancy, Arthur, and Spencer to race. Even the family dog, Clover, is put to the test, although Clover usually prefers to tackle Taylor than race.

"When she jumps on me," Taylor says, "I win."

Taylor is not at all fussy about clothes, but she does take her white pair of Fila sneakers seriously.

"They always come undone and the tongue's always going to one side or another and I have to push it back down the middle," Taylor says. "I go faster in them."

As Taylor sprints across the school playground or the soccer field, with her legs motoring in measured strides, it seems so natural, a gift.

Her black waist-length ponytail, swinging from side to side as she weaves between the swing sets and the basketball court, only heightens the effect. She even stops fast. In an instant, she can pivot in any direction, as first her arms, then her hips, legs, and feet follow the path first determined by her eyes.

Watch closer though, and you begin to see there is something more than a girl with a gift. Taylor is using her eyes. Her head and chest are arched back just so. Her lips are sealed with determination. There is total focus. As she runs, Taylor is also thinking.

Lately, Taylor has become obsessed with time. She doesn't run miles on the track. Instead, she has backyard and playground courses that she repeats. In addition to her after-school runs, Nancy and Arthur must time dashes between soccer goalposts and trees. In the backyard, it is nine seconds to the picnic table.

When Arthur and Nancy took her to a science museum there was an exhibit about running the hundred-yard dash. Taylor carefully studied the countdown and position of the feet in the starting blocks.

She is only seven, but she is figuring things out.

"My arms move around and help me go a little faster," she says. "If they keep out straight, then I'll go slower."

Champions are born, and they are made.

Taylor has a gift. She will be the one to unwrap it.

CHAPTER 21

The DAWN PATROL

Finding friendship in a new hometown

One by one, the women gather under a streetlamp on a silent suburban corner. It is a little before five on a misty Carolina morning. The sky is as gray and lumpy as an old woolen blanket. The air is sweet with the scent of wet honeysuckle. Sheila pulls into a parking spot and hops out of her van. Liz, wearing an orange vest with reflector strips, waits at the curb, talking to Gina. Pat, a schoolteacher due in her kindergarten classroom in two hours, stands with Janet, a hospital administrator in charge of a hundred employees.

Everyone whispers. The last time they gathered for their dawn run, a neighbor stormed out of her house. "Every morning you women wake me up!" she scolded. The runners try hard not to make noise, stifling laughs like schoolgirls. After the last of the group arrives, the dozen women scamper into the darkness—and crank up the volume.

You could set your watch to the Dawn Patrol. By 5 A.M. sharp, they're off for a forty-five-minute run, winding in and out of the empty streets of surrounding developments, or sometimes running intervals on the deserted track at the nearby middle school. While their children and husbands slumber, the women will log almost five miles of running, as well as a daily dose of friendship.

Strangers once, the women have turned their early-morning jogs into an enduring ritual. And it all started when Sheila Burgard moved to Chapel Hill, North Carolina, and went hunting for friends.

Sheila was accustomed to moving around a lot with her husband. She met Ed in Bethesda, Maryland, in the 1980s, while they worked at the same medical center. Sheila was a bio-statistician; Ed, a pharmacologist. They hopscotched from the Deep South to the Midwest as Ed's training took him first to the University of Alabama in Birmingham, then to the University of Michigan in Ann Arbor. Their next stop: Libertyville, Illinois, a bedroom community north of Chicago. Ed had a good research job with a big drug maker. Sheila started to think of Libertyville as home. Their neighborhood was tight. Everyone had front porches, and when the weather turned warm, coolers came out and the invitation was open to stop and chat for an evening.

After 9/11, with the economy slumping, Ed kept his eyes open for work options. A friend working in North Carolina's booming biotech industry reached out to him. "No harm in taking a look," Ed thought.

"I knew change was coming," Sheila can say now. Even so, she wasn't ready when Ed returned from North Carolina, convinced they should move. She fell apart. "Until then, I had done a good job of hiding my fear," Sheila recalls.

Once again, boxes were packed, family pictures taken down from the walls, promises made to neighbors and schoolmates to stay in touch. And once again, Sheila and her brood found themselves in a new town—this time the community of Carrboro, just outside Chapel Hill.

No kid likes to start all over again with a new school, new friends, and new neighbors. And guess what? No mom likes it either. It took only two days for Sheila's son to discover a boy his age two doors away. Her daughter settled into fourth grade, while her youngest girl was content to stay by mom's side.

Sheila, on the other hand, felt lost. She would see other women when she dropped off the kids at school, just a few blocks away. But parking lot chatter among the pickup moms rarely went deeper than that. One morning, soon after the school year started, Sheila went for a run in her neighborhood. A couple of blocks ahead, she saw a short jogger. She recognized the woman as one of the moms from pickup time at school. Sheila started to sprint. "I chased her," says Sheila, plain and simple. By the time she caught up with the other woman, she blurted out in one breathless stream, *"I saw you at school . . . we just moved here . . . can I run along?"*

Gina Lacava laughs when she hears Sheila tell the story. "I chased *you,*" she insists. Like Sheila, Gina was also a newcomer, isolated at home with kids. They agreed to meet early the next morning. Gina had just started running with another neighbor, Cindy. Sheila joined them.

In the months ahead, Sheila recruited other moms from school. So did Gina. Turns out the neighborhood was filled with women just like them. Between the University of North Carolina and all the new biotech companies, the area was a magnet for transplants, arriving without the safety net of family and friends.

Koreen had just relocated from the Washington, D.C., area. Jen was uprooted from New Jersey. Liz was a Miami native, who pined for her Florida family and friends. Like the others, she saw her running circle as an anchor. "This is constant and solid," Liz explains.

When Pat, a teacher, joined the group, she asked if they could begin earlier. They pushed the start time back to 5:45 A.M. No one complained. They all had kids to get off to school or jobs to run to. The earlier, the better. Eventually, they settled on a 5 A.M. rendezvous.

Sheila savored her morning runs. She found herself connecting with new, interesting people, forging friendships that usually don't come so easily at that stage of life. If there was any doubt that the others felt the same, Sheila need only recall the Christmas Eve morning, early in the life of the group. She woke and looked out the window at a heavy, wet snow. "No one in their right mind will show up today," Sheila thought as she nevertheless put on her sweats and laced her shoes. "I must be crazy to think we'll run." Liz Buchman had her doubts, too, as she dressed to run. It was Christmas Eve after all. "I'm Jewish and I bet I'm the only one who'll show up," she convinced herself. When both of them got to the meeting spot, a dozen runners were waiting under the streetlamp. "It was a miracle," Sheila says.

There's an easy answer for why the Dawn Patrol is still running after so many years. The women know something that all runners come to understand. The image of the distance runner is the lone figure in a solitary battle for speed and endurance. But running is actually one of the most communal sports. "We're pack animals, we really are," Sheila laughs. And the more runners talk, the easier it feels. Sure, you can chat during a round of golf or between sets of tennis. But imagine trying to keep up a conversation as your golf partner lines up a putt or during an intense volley at the net. With running, on the other hand, the deeper the talk goes, the more the pain eases. But there are rules about what you hear on the road, as Liz Buchman explains: "We always say leave it on the road."

The running group has become a movable village, where

women swap advice on matters small and large, from issues as mundane as helping a baby sleep through the night to crises as grave as a hospitalized child. For Liz, the Florida native, the women were her lifeline when her six-year-old son came down with a rare form of cancer. With her family in Florida and her husband just as weary and confused as she was, Liz leaned on her friends. They were supportive, she now sees, in a way that her siblings and mother probably couldn't be. Instead of telling her what to do, as relatives would do, they listened. Pat Karrigan, she says, was a rock. As they ran, Liz would pour out her fears and confusion over the bewildering maze of medical tests, treatments, and decisions. And after their run, Pat would hurry home, shower, and head to work—teaching Liz's son in kindergarten. After chemotherapy, the boy had to be home-schooled for two months. Every day, Pat checked on him and Liz. Without being asked, the other runners brought Liz meals.

This, Liz explains, is what keeps the women rising before dawn to run through the streets together, the murmur of their conversation rising above the neighborhood stillness. For forty-five minutes before another hectic day begins, the women will laugh a little, talk a lot, ponder the mysteries of children and husbands, analyze everything from movies to food, while dispensing help on matters of health, finance, and home. "It's like a girls' night out every time we run," explains Koreen Billman, a mother of three.

And come the morning, they'll be back for more.

Acknowledgments

Writing a book, we have learned, is a lot like running a marathon. We'd like to thank our supporters on the sidelines— kids and spouses, coworkers and siblings—who kept us going.

Thanks to Jennifer Unter, our agent from RLR Associates in New York, who endorsed our idea from the get-go and never gave up. To photographer Andrea Mihalik, whose images of women runners capture the spirit of *Sole Sisters*. And to essayist Hugh O'Neill, who nudged us into bookwriting by asking not "Why?" but "Why not?"

Special gratitude to Bill Stieg, the word doctor, whose unerring sense of a well-told story and skill at polishing prose made this a better book.

We acknowledge, too, the runners who understood our mission, steered us to subjects, and encouraged us: Susan Pajer, Ann Cutrell, the Lin sisters and nieces, Wendy Body, Ellen Wessel, and Judy West. And mostly, we'd like to thank all the women and girls who so graciously and generously shared their stories when we reached out to them—sometimes out of the blue—and asked, "Why do you run?"